MINDING THE GIRAFFES

The People Side of Innovation

JOHN DI FRANCES

RELIANCE BOOKS — WALES, WISCONSIN

PUBLISHED IN THE U.S.A.

Reliance Books

Email: Contact@RelianceBooks.com

Website: http://www.RelianceBooks.com

ORDERING INFORMATION

Quantity Sales: Special discounts are available on quantity purchases by corporations, educational institutions, government units, associations, churches and some other qualifying groups.   For details contact the 'Special Sales' department or see our website.

Individual Sales: Reliance books publications are available at many bookstores as well as on Amazon.com. They can also be ordered directly from Reliance Books.

Printed in The United States of America.

Di Frances, John
Minding the giraffes: the people side of innovation / John Di Frances

p. cm.
Includes biographical references.

Library of Congress Control Number: 2012951611
ISBN-13: 978-0-9709908-3-9 (paperback)
ISBN-13: 978-0-9709908-4-7 (e-book)
1. Innovation. 2. Creativity in business. 3. Organizational change. 4. Leadership.

Editor: Sarah (Sally) Webber
Assisting Editors: Christy Di Frances, PhD and Jamie Grim
Cover Design by Annie Melrose

To all those who had a hand in making this book possible, both family and friends, for your steadfast encouragement and participation during the writing and long months of editing and refining which followed. 'What is worth doing is worth doing right.'

Other Books by John Di Frances

Reclaiming the Ethical High Ground: Developing Organizations of Character

JackBilt® a Company: Of Happy, Successful People

I saw the angel in the marble and carved until I set him free.

– Michelangelo

Contents

PART I   The Quest for Innovation

PART II   Giraffes to the Rescue

Acknowledgments

Without my dedicated editor, Sally, this book may never have come into existence. Although an interest in innovation began early in my career, it was she who suggested, 'Your next book needs to be about innovation. Call it *Minding the Giraffes*.' As she is a Giraffe of a different color, her mind is always at work. In conversation, it is not unusual for her to suddenly change the subject and interject what seems to me a completely random, unrelated comment. While for her, it is simply an unannounced detour.

I have great difficulty following such apparently mid-thought subject changes but that makes us even, as I consistently do the same in my writing (or so she tells me), which complicates her task of editing. I write at a machine gun pace where a chapter a day is not unusual. From my perspective, the thoughts flow seamlessly, but she often informs me that this is not the case and cavernous presumptions lurk in between, poised to swallow up unsuspecting readers. She then labors to bridge what has just been said with what ought to come next, filling in the logic so very obvious to me. Fortunately, she is as much a creative writer in her own right as an editor and accepts the challenge.

So Sally, this book is dedicated to Giraffes like you! Thank you for making this book possible through your title idea and many strenuous efforts in 'connecting the dots.'

I would also like to thank Annie Melrose for her distinctive cover design.

For real innovation to thrive, everyone has to be on one team with common objectives and goals, staying focused on the common good of the organization and everyone in it.

Foreword

Most business leaders today understand that the way of the past will not be the way of the future. The growing influence of technology, globalization and national economic strains continues to change the marketplace for all businesses, whether local or international. The paradigms and solutions that organizations counted on in the past to grow and prosper are no longer viable.

Minding the Giraffes is indispensable reading for navigating these troubled times where everyone is seeking sustainable growth. This book zeros in on the people who generate breakthrough ideas, and leadership's role in developing an on-going culture of innovation.

Through valuable content as well as a fascinating trek into the animal realm, John Di Frances examines strategic innovation from a nonconventional perspective. He explains that innovation is much more than a given formula or philosophy. To succeed in building businesses that are innovation driven, we must shift our focus to the *'People Side of Innovation.'*

John answers the question of how to build on the abilities of *Giraffe Innovators* — individuals possessing a natural gift for innovation. John contends that breakthrough innovation is within our reach when we facilitate the efforts of those who 'see' what is possible and operate outside of established thinking patterns. We begin to understand that innovation cannot be successfully achieved without the full support of leadership in each phase of development as well as cross-organizationally. He emphasizes that true innovators are passionate about what they do and need to see their innovations realized.

John Di Frances counsels business leaders to pay heed to the innovators and take steps to empower them. In a turbulent, technology driven economy, new *ideas* are definitely the way forward. ***Minding the Giraffes*** provides the courage to see things differently and the confidence to succeed through strategic innovation.

- Eisuke.Tsuyuzaki, Chief Technical Officer, Panasonic (North America)

GOAL

This book is the first in a series intended to change mindsets and broaden the understanding of innovation — what it is, how it occurs, and how to nurture and instill it within organizations.

Understanding Innovation Series

Book I - The People of Innovation - *Minding the Giraffes*

Book II - The Leadership of Innovation

Book III - The Process of Innovation

Book IV - The Product of Innovation

PRINCIPLES OF CHANGE

1. Giving People a Vision of What Can Be

2. Establishing Values by Which That Vision Becomes Reality

3. Empowering People to Realize the Vision

These were the principles practiced by William Wilberforce, who through a decades long struggle in Parliament was instrumental in the abolition of the British slave trade – and later of slavery itself throughout the British Empire.

Giraffes are truly the primary agents of innovation.

PART I   The Quest for Innovation

Why You Should Read the Preface

Many people believe that reading a book's Preface is a waste of time. That may be so in some instances, but definitely NOT here!

Skip the Preface and you will miss some imperative information regarding the central theme and purpose of *Minding the Giraffes*.

What does innovation have to do with giraffes? The Preface solves this mystery and sets the premise for the book.

So, please read it!

Without the Giraffes, it is quite possible that no one will be asking the question, 'Why?'

Preface:
Giraffes and the Question, *'Why?'*

'Why?' Why is it done this way - why not that way? *'Why?'* is a question that always forces us to think. It demands our attention and inconveniently requires an intelligent and thoughtful answer. It pulls the rug out from under us so that we cannot help but look at what lies beneath. When raised, it more often than not exposes glaring problems.

Rather than focus on the disruptive nature of *'Why?'* – let us consider in a more positive light, the disruptor, the person posing the questions. Given the challenges of an unforgiving global economy, it may be time to regard that person as more of a resource than a nuisance. For that individual may be gifted not only with the ability to unearth difficulties, but the capacity to 'see' and create innovative solutions which could revolutionize the future of your organization.

Every new pursuit begins with the question, *'Why?'* It captures the imagination and sets into motion a quest for the solutions needed to realize an idea, seize an opportunity, solve a problem, or create something entirely new. Whether for businesses, government agencies, or not-for-profits, *'Why?'* sparks the ideation process, lending momentum to every task we undertake or innovation we seek to achieve.

But, why is this question so frequently left unasked? In the urgency and crush of management responsibility, the essential role of critical inquiry is often swept aside. Worse yet, in some organizations, asking *'Why?'* could prove perilous to an otherwise promising career. Whether the function is R&D, Marketing, Accounting, Finance, Strategic Planning, Production, Sales, Maintenance, HR, Purchasing, Customer Service or any of the diverse functions defining modern organizations, *'Why?'* needs to be at the forefront of everyone's thinking – inspiring discussion in every meeting, lunchroom, and hallway conversation. This crucial question should be welcomed everywhere from our boardrooms to entry level cubicles and the shop floor.

The shop floor? Absolutely. If 'Imagination is more important than knowledge,' as Einstein suggested, then we are underestimating its potential. Of course, we need knowledge. But knowledge is limited, while imagination is not. The ability to visualize and generate ideas is not the sole domain of the highly educated.

Think of the whiz kid who drops out of college freshman year. Or consider an example of crowd sourcing that took place during World War II, when 200,000 ideas were submitted to the National Inventors' Council in hopes of aiding the war effort. These ideas came from people of all walks of life, including factory workers, between 1942 and 1945. Many which initially seemed implausible were later implemented by the Department of Defense to help the armed forces and hasten the war's end.

What prevents us from 'seeing' simple and obvious solutions today? Established patterns of thinking, our entrenched paradigms. Our actions are too often limited by our perception of a fixed reality, whereas true innovators are always seeking new approaches.

Clinging to conventional thinking and methods is especially dangerous in a fast-shifting marketplace where you can be blindsided by a competitor's innovations. And this is hardly an aberration, as every day static business models fall victim to the bombardment of innovative ideas which continually redefine the marketplace rules of engagement. Turning a blind eye and a deaf ear to the question, *'Why?'* – and with it the call to innovate – is a principal reason so many organizations struggle in today's economy.

Giraffes to the Rescue

This book examines that peculiar minority who live and breathe 'ideas' and, despite clear consequences, create controversy by asking uncomfortable questions. I have called these unconventional thinkers Giraffes with a capital G, not to be confused with the animals found roaming across Africa or capturing the astonished gazes of children at the local zoo.

Giraffe innovators are the most imaginative members of the business world because they are the people who generate ideas — the kind of game-changing ideas that forever alter the marketplace. They are essential players in the successful cultivation of an organization-wide culture of innovation for the purpose of achieving breakthrough change.

I have included several examples of successful innovation which I spearheaded on behalf of a previous employer and clients of my consulting firm. This is to illustrate how suddenly and in what strange ways opportunities for real innovation can arise. It is a mistake to think that we can systematize and regiment innovation. The moment we seek to do so, we have lost the genius that is innovation. If we expect innovation to serve us, we must always be open to it, even when it is least expected or most inconvenient. We must remain open to the possibility that we may have been wrong – completely and utterly wrong in our viewpoints, approaches, methods and thinking. Innovation can be a generous rewarder of the bold, but we must be prepared to run the gauntlet in terms of hard work, fear, and risk to win those rewards. Innovation is not for the faint-hearted, neither is it for those who place comfort above the challenge of achieving great outcomes.

At the end of each chapter of this book, I have included an example of an outstanding Giraffe innovator. These individuals are drawn from a broad range of fields and educational backgrounds, both contemporary and historical, in order to demonstrate the diversity and reach of their influence on society. Some fascinating data on actual giraffes, the namesakes of our Giraffe innovators, has also been woven throughout the book for your enjoyment. You will discover some amazing facts about giraffes, as I draw interesting parallels between these marvelous creatures and their human counterparts.

I have also included 'Thought Questions' at the end of each chapter. Take time to read and consider them, either individually or as a group activity, if you are part of a team that is reading this book. Getting through the book quickly is not the goal. Learning from it and applying what you learn to your organization is the goal.

This book will help you understand why every business needs Giraffes. Without the Giraffes, it is quite possible that no one will be asking the question *'Why?'* Giraffes are truly the primary agents of innovation.

Preface Thought Questions

1. Is it my goal to daily ask the question *'Why?'* and encourage those who report to me to do likewise?

2. As individuals and an organization, how can we encourage the agents of innovation, those who ask *'Why?'* and prevent them from being regarded as troublemakers?

3. What typically occurs when someone interrupts a meeting's planned agenda by challenging the basis of an action, policy or procedure we are discussing by asking *'Why?'*

4. How receptive am I and the organization to new ideas and solutions which are unfamiliar and untested?

5. Do we see innovation as a responsibility of R&D alone or do we welcome it regardless of origin, anticipating that every department and function will actively and continuously seek innovation?

Innovation keeps changing the game.

Chapter One: Why Innovation?

Ultimately, innovation is the only sustainable strategy for long term growth and profitability.

For the past decade, innovation has become the darling buzzword of the business world. In fact, you rarely see an issue of *Fast Company* or any other business magazine for that matter without a feature article or at least, significant reference to the topic of innovation. Books and articles on the subject abound. Government leaders, from presidents and prime ministers to local politicians, sprinkle the word like sugar over countless statements and campaign speeches.

Corporate executives tout commitments for their companies to become innovation leaders while a seemingly endless army of consultants and advisors profess expertise on the subject. The commercial arena is simply saturated with the talk of innovation.

This sounds wonderful. At least it would be, if the net result was an explosion of *real innovation*. Unfortunately, in actuality, innovation is not spontaneously erupting around the globe. While it is true that innovation has the capacity to revitalize businesses and other types of organizations, despite all the glitter and hype, real innovation is happening less often today than before the term came into vogue.

To a great extent, the 'genuine article' has been lost in all the ballyhoo. How is this possible, when so many powerful and well-placed people repeatedly extol the immense potential of innovation?

The answer lies in the fact that few of its most vocal enthusiasts have any real clue about what innovation actually is – and even fewer possess a grasp of how to harness its power to make it a driving force to benefit their organizations. If that seems harsh, I can only say that it is the assessment of a decades-long career of teaching, mentoring, and creating real innovation.

So, what is innovation? The following definition by Peter Drucker is accurate and brief:

'Change that creates a new dimension of performance.'

How often does your organization produce that magnitude of change? If it doesn't do so frequently, why not? In a global economy, without regular breakthroughs which create new dimensions of performance, you cannot and will not remain viable in your marketplace.

Innovation that results in a real change in scope and dimension, enhancing tangible performance, is not 'alive and well' in most organizations today. As a result of a failure to voice the critical question, *'Why?'* or rather, *'Why not?'* global competition and a fast-shifting economy threaten sustainability. Whole industries have witnessed their markets evaporating before their very eyes, too slow to realize that in today's marketplace, change is the only constant, change occurring at an accelerating pace. We must learn to implement continuous innovation for it is our best and only defense.

When was the last time you had your car's engine tuned-up? Not that many years ago, a tune-up was recommended by auto manufacturers every 10,000 or 20,000 miles. Now, for most cars, it's every 100,000 miles. Times change. If you own an auto repair shop today, you had better not be counting on engine tune-ups to keep your business profitable.

For those who have been frequent flyers for more than a decade or two, can you recall the days when you would dash off the airplane hoping to find a phone carousel just beyond the jetway? When is the last time you looked for a pay phone at the airport to make a call? When is the last time you saw a pay telephone…anywhere? Innovation keeps changing the game.

What about your home telephone, if you even have a land-line at home anymore? Telephone companies were among the most secure businesses in existence, until the federally mandated break-up of 'Ma Bell,' which took place in 1984. Then came the cable TV companies, offering not only TV programming minus an aerial, but also high speed wireless internet and home telephone service in a bundle.

The land-line telephone companies retaliated with customer packages offering wired or satellite TV programming and high speed internet together with wired telephone service. The two competing groups began driving down prices – and with them each other's margins.

Today, they are all in jeopardy, as 'Over-the-Top' TV boxes such as Roku and Boxee offer access to a wide range of TV programing, while NetFlix, Blockbuster and a host of others proffer a nearly unlimited range of downloadable and streaming movies. Add to the fray Apple TV, Google TV, and the latest entry, Aereo, which provide programming directly over the internet at very competitive prices. If that isn't enough, additional competitors such as Intel are preparing to flood the market with a bevy of new product offerings.

At the same time, a proliferation of DVR recorders is allowing the public to record programs for viewing, at their convenience, days, weeks or even months later. This plays havoc with the Nielsen program ratings as well as the efforts of advertisers airing time sensitive programming and product promotions. To make matters worse, technology now enables viewers to 'skip' all of the ads for seamless programming.

And what of the other services Cable TV and traditional telephone companies offer? The future of land-line telephone businesses is at best 'shaky' as more and more people choose to cut the cord. For the first time, the second quarter of 2012 saw a decline in cable subscribers. If you have adult children living on their own, consider how few still have a land-line telephone. And what about the Baby-Boomer generation? Typically far slower to adapt to technological change, a surprising number have followed suit, abandoning the land line corded phone.

Many small businesses are now opting for cell-only phone service. Most new business start-ups are, after all, one or two person operations. And once they begin growing, it makes sense to add more cell phones, as there is little differential in cost and their personnel can be more accessible to customer calls, whether in or out of the office.

And there are more twists to come in this trend of cutting the cable. As large corporations gravitate to more flexible work environments with work from home days, full time work at home personnel, flexible offices, etc., will major corporations continue to maintain large land-line phone systems? Probably, but will the number of land-lines they pay for each month grow or even remain steady? Most likely, they will shrink. I speak with business executives on a daily basis and am amazed by how many of them do not even bother to give me their office phone number, opting instead for a cell phone number, particularly if they are in sales, marketing, or other functions that keep them out of the office much of the time.

What then of the third prong of the cable and phone industry's offering: wired high speed internet access? At least, that must be safe. Not really. In the near future a rapidly growing number of people will begin cutting the cable here, too. Their rationale? A burgeoning market of mobile devices. While you may have a 72+ inch flat screen TV adorning your living room wall with several others in the 40-50" range scattered throughout your home, now you can have all the programming you want, up close and personal, anytime and anywhere you want on your iPad, iPhone or similar mobile device. After all, mobile devices don't use a wall jack and cable to reach the internet. They are designed to be exclusively Wifi. So why bother having a wire and router? Increasingly, mobile wifi service reaches wherever you go, particularly in large metropolitan areas where free public wifi networks are becoming the trend.

In short, it is no longer necessary to be at home, the office, or a wired coffee shop to connect to the internet. A park bench or, better yet, the beach offers very attractive alternatives. Nor has the advantage of this opportunity been lost to mobile service providers such as AT&T and Verizon. The push to fulfill the public's insatiable appetite for connectivity will work against the land-line companies as mobile wireless companies offering 'everywhere connectivity' provide consumers with increasingly better and more cost-effective wireless solutions.

The unnerving result is that a utility company business model, which until just recently appeared rock solid, is now being challenged in all three of its core markets: wired TV, telephone, and internet access.

However, there are signs of hope that the industry is beginning to wake up and act innovatively. Verizon and TimeWarner Cable have entered into a cross-marketing agreement that allows them to bundle and cross-sell the services of both companies to their customers. This is, at least, a small step in the right direction.

I referenced AT&T above, but it is not the behemoth American Telephone & Telegraph Company many of us remember. The present AT&T began as a landline telephone company, Southwestern Bell Corporation, one of the seven original regional Bell operating companies that reinvented itself as a wireless carrier. In 1995, it changed its name to SBC Communications, Inc. Then, in 2005, SBC bought its former parent company, AT&T, thus acquiring the powerful AT&T brand name. Today, only the trade name 'AT&T' has endured, not the once formidable 'AT&T' which essentially became obsolete.

Like a mighty steamroller, innovation keeps changing the business landscape. The cable and telephone industries are far from alone. Consider one of the oldest and stodgiest businesses: the book publishing industry. In a matter of mere months, venerable names in publishing have suddenly realized the world has passed them by and unless they can pull a proverbial 'rabbit' out of their hat, many will not survive.

What happened here? A 'perfect storm' of factors brewing for years and then, suddenly bursting over them with the 'shock and awe' we thought only the U.S. military could inflict. First, a sharp decline in book reading among the general population in favor of other sources of knowledge and entertainment. That, together with the phenomenal success of Amazon.com rising to become the undisputed book sales Goliath, unfortunately triggered the closing of many small bookstores which were unable to compete with the Amazon model and large chain book stores. In the 1998 hit movie *You've Got Mail,* starring Tom Hanks and Meg Ryan, you may recall the demise of the charming 'Shop Around the Corner' independent bookstore soon after the 'evil' Fox Books megastore chain appeared just around *their* corner.

Then came the death of B. Dalton Books, one of the three mega bookstore chains. In 2011, Borders Books followed suit, having had six CEO's during the period of 1999 to its final demise. Just one of their failed strategies was the opening of fourteen 'concept stores' in 2008, that were even more massive than their regular stores. The center-point of these new stores were 'download stations' where customers could purchase and download books and music. As late as 2008, Border's executives seemed to have missed the crucial point that 'downloading' was something that customers do from their home, office or the local coffee shop while surfing the net and not a reason to drive to their store. Barnes & Noble gobbled up the remnants of Border's on-line business, the only asset with an on-going value.

Meanwhile, e-books are wrestling market share from publishers and traditional bookstores alike, fueled by the growing demand for a cheap alternative to high priced, newly released hardcovers. Add to this a throng of hungry authors, some of them very good and thoroughly frustrated with trying to break into a publishing citadel guarded by an alliance of elitist editors and agents, many of whom seem be less concerned about seeing good books reach readers than protecting their own territory. Even J.K. Rowling, author of the blockbuster Harry Potter series, who after enjoying tremendous success and reaping a vast fortune with her publisher, has started Pottermore, her own publishing company setting the industry on its head and encouraging other well established authors to create their own imprint. A headline in the *Huffington Post* read, 'The J.K. Rowling's Effect - Traditional Publishing Takes Another Blow to the Head,' recounts how big name authors are following her lead into the world of 'indie' (self-publishing).

The coup de grâce was the invasion of Amazon into the publishing market. After all, why shouldn't the world's largest book seller integrate vertically into book publishing? Amazon executives must have been asking themselves the question *'Why not?'* They were already offering e-book self-publishing, giving unknown authors an unprecedented quick and inexpensive route into the market. Simply begin by taking the best selling e-books and publishing them in printed form as well, using fast and efficient print-on-demand technology. Today, when you order a print-on-demand title from Amazon, it is printed and shipped within two to three days, not just business days, but seven days a week. And it is never 'Out of Stock.'

Thus, a 'perfect storm' has engulfed the entire book publishing marketplace. And there will be no turning back the clock, no matter how desperately established players may wish for a second chance at survival.

To date, the reaction of industry giants to this sudden market upheaval is apparently denial. An article in *Bloomberg Businessweek* entitled 'The Match Isn't Over Yet' points this out:

> Publishers worry that a widespread shift to print on demand could, like the advent of e-books, disrupt their century-old business model. Companies such as Random House and Simon & Schuster have spent decades investing in their own supply chains, storing books in giant warehouses and developing the transportation infrastructure to ship those volumes to stores within days. If print on demand became widespread, publishers could cut their fixed cost and solve the perennial problem of stores returning unsold books. But that would

throw into doubt almost everything else about the way big publishers conduct business, since they're compensated based on the range of services they provide, from editorial guidance to storage and distribution. Print-on-demand technology would make it harder for the publishers to justify keeping a large majority of a book's wholesale price.

Does something about this statement raise any red flags? For example, '... disrupt their century-old business model.' Welcome to the 21st century, where the new norm is disruption! Possibly the only other industry to proudly share a 'cast-in-stone' century-old business model is higher education, and even that is changing. Why has the book publishing industry been so determined to protect an outdated business model? The culprit is short-sighted self-interest – always the enemy of innovation, thwarting and frustrating the course of progress. If the book publishing industry had been mindful to innovate all along, there would be no need to worry about how to 'justify keeping a large majority of a book's wholesale price.' In which case, business would be booming and authors receiving their *fair* share of book sale profits.

The article continues:

> As the digital transition upends the industry, resistance to on-demand printing may fade. Smaller publishers that have already made the switch away from printing and storing their own books say it's well worth it. 'Instead of putting all those books in a warehouse, you free up cash flow to invest in R&D,' says Laura Baldwin, president of O'Reilly Media, a publisher of technical books that moved to print on demand last year and shed $1.6 million in inventory cost. 'You can invest in the technical future of publishing as opposed to printed books that are sitting in the warehouse.'

On yet another publishing front, Newsweek magazine, after eighty years, is ending publication of its print edition. It will be an online only subscription magazine renamed Newsweek Global. Tina Brown, Editor-in-Chief, characterized the move as bowing to the inevitable digital future. 'You cannot actually change an era of enormous disruptive innovation,' she stated. 'No one single person can reverse that trend. You can't turn back what is an inexorable trend.'

But marketplace disruptions are hardly limited to these industries alone. As resources tighten and the world becomes increasingly globalized, every organization risks being blind-sided.   A hungry competitor with a flair for innovation, a player from totally outside your marketplace who seizes upon a sudden window of opportunity, or maybe even a 'whiz kid' who just dropped out of college to try his or her hand at becoming the next billionaire entrepreneur – all pose the same very real threat to established organizations. A threat which may not even begin in your industry. An earth-shaking innovation originating in an entirely different industry or marketplace can create a tsunami… sweeping others away without warning.

'Why Innovation?' In an era of accelerating change, innovation is the only viable strategy for sustainable growth.

Giraffe Example:

Sir Richard Charles Nicholas Branson

My interest in life comes from setting myself huge, apparently unachievable challenges and trying to rise above them...from the perspective of wanting to live life to the full, I felt that I had to attempt it.

A serial entrepreneur who has become one of the wealthiest people in his native England, Sir Richard Charles Nicholas Branson is flamboyant, controversial, and at times enigmatic — he is also a true Giraffe innovator.

Born on July 18, 1950, Branson is best known for his Virgin Group of worldwide companies, which now number over 400. His first business venture, begun at the age of sixteen, was the publication of a magazine called *Student* from a church crypt. He followed this in 1970 with a mail-order music record business, which he operated from the same unique location. Branson used the magazine to advertise popular records.

In 1972, he founded a chain of retail brick and mortar record stores which he called Virgin Records. 'Virgin' was suggested as the business name by one of Branson's first employees, because all of the entrepreneurs involved were 'virgins' at business. Branson pioneered the discounting of music recordings which would later set a precedent for the music industry. Eventually, Virgin stores diversified to offer a wide array of merchandise and were renamed Virgin Megastores. Interestingly, Branson acknowledges that it was Steve Job's foray into the music industry with the iPod, that signaled the demise of the Virgin record stores.

The Virgin brand continued to expand with the founding of Virgin Atlantic Airways Limited, better known as Virgin Atlantic, in 1984. In order to keep his airline company afloat, Branson sold the Virgin record label for £500 million in 1992. Branson recounts to having wept when the sale was completed, as the company represented the 'birth' of the Virgin Empire. In 1996, Branson launched V2 Records to replace the music business he had been forced to sell years earlier.

When, in 1993, the government-owned British train system was in the midst of privatization, Branson acquired a segment of British Rail and embarked upon what may have been his highest-risk business endeavor up to then with the formation of Virgin Trains. In 1996, he purchased Euro Belgian Airlines, a short haul European carrier, which he renamed Virgin Express. He later went on to found Virgin Nigeria, an Africa-based national airline.

In 1999, Branson launched the Virgin Mobile phone company and in 2000 founded yet another airline, Virgin Blue, in Australia (which was later renamed Virgin Australia). This was followed by the debut of the Virgin America airline in 2007.

Among Branson's various businesses, a few were unsuccessful: for instance, the Virgin Cola and Virgin Vodka brands. Innovation entails serial risk taking and every innovator will experience failures as well as successes. One of his most avant-garde ventures was announced in September 2004, with the founding of Virgin Galactic, a space tourism company formed to take paying passengers into suborbital space for a target fare of $200,000. Other business endeavors have included Virgin Media, Virgin Comics, Virgin Health Bank, Virgin Fuels, Virgin Earth Challenge and Virgin (auto) Racing. Charles Branson is undoubtedly an innovator par excellence!

Chapter 1 — Thought Questions

1. Why is 'innovation' the ultimate strategy?

2. How often does our organization produce real innovation, *Change that creates a new dimension of performance?*

3. What is meant by a 'new dimension of performance.'

4. Do we frequently reassess the risk factors produced by others, both inside and outside of our industry, creating innovations which could blindside us?

5. Are we clinging to an out-dated business model?

6. What are the global change factors that represent the greatest risks to our organization's future? Do we even know what they are?

7. Is there an alternative strategy to innovation that can assure a sustainable future for our organization?

8. Does Branson strike us as being 'safe'?

9. What do record stores, mega stores, airline companies, comics, media companies, health companies, auto racing and space travel have in common?

10. Would Branson fit and prosper in our organization?

Innovation is not a simple process produced through a rote series of cookie-cutter steps.

Chapter Two: Why Giraffes?

In nature, Giraffes are the tallest animal on earth, with grown males reaching heights of 20 feet. Their height enables them to see a full panorama of the horizon in the spacious grasslands where they live. Giraffes are endowed with extremely keen eyesight and a wide field of peripheral vision. These attributes allow them to see danger while it is still far away and spot prime locations for food and water. Extraordinary eyesight, together with their unusually long necks, makes giraffes the 'eagle' of ground-based mammals.

Giraffe innovators are also keen visionaries. In business, innovation is an imperative strategy for survival and profitable growth. Because every organization possesses limited resources in terms of talent, time, and money, the ability to see ahead, above and beyond others, enables an organization's leadership to correctly allocate their resources into those innovation efforts that have the greatest likelihood of producing exponential results — namely, the biggest bang for the buck!

Every organization needs access to the capabilities of Giraffes. The creativity they generate is essential to profitable growth and continued marketplace relevance. Innovation is not a simple process produced through a rote series of cookie-cutter steps. Too often, management becomes fixated on following a given system or methodology for innovation that someone may have read about. Unfortunately, there is no set formula for achieving innovation. Innovation may begin with an inspiration, but the follow through involves a combination of hard work, problem solving, and *risk*.

Innovation is not *safe*! I advise executives that if the majority, 80% or more, of their organization's innovation initiatives do not fail, they are not really innovating — not stretching the envelope nearly far enough. However, one real innovation can far more than offset the cost of numerous failed attempts. Once again, I am not advocating that organizations normally take risks in innovations which 'bet the ranch.' Do you recall the definition of Innovation provided in the last chapter?

'Change that creates a new dimension of performance.'

You cannot continually produce new dimensions of performance by playing it safe. Now and then, innovation can occur by accident, but that is a fluke rather than a consistent business model. The *new* in new dimensions presupposes a significant degree of the *unknown* – and the unknown is never safe. Let's take a closer look at the definition of innovation and its five key words:

Change — Dramatic transformation from one state to another. The key is that something becomes *dramatically different*. Real Innovation is not usually incremental or evolutionary in nature. It is *radical*!

Creates — Originates, generates, brings into being within the context of a specific application.

New — Novel, fresh, imaginative, cutting-edge — or even bleeding-edge — correlating with, or even exceeding, the rate of change surrounding the organization and its marketplaces.

Dimension — Aspect, facet, magnitude.

Performance — Capacity, power, potential.

Dramatic Change typically goes against the organizational grain. It is disruptive. Organizations are more likely to embrace change that is evolutionary, because it is slow and predictable, requiring low risk and only a marginal threshold of challenge to the status quo. It is far easier to adapt to incremental or evolutionary change. Dramatic change is anything but slow, predictable and safe; nevertheless, it has the power to reposition you in the marketplace whereas incremental or evolutionary change cannot.

The same applies to *new*, *novel*, *fresh*, *imaginative*, *cutting-edge*, and *bleeding-edge*. These words strike fear into the hearts of many, especially in long established executive and managerial ranks.

Giraffes are those very rare individuals who are comfortable with terms like **cutting-edge** and **bleeding-edge** — as well as their implications. The Giraffe's concept of capitalism is founded on a premise of risk and reward. However, as organizations grow and become more firmly entrenched, the reward aspect is emphasized while the risk aspect is deliberately minimized. Just look at the trend of many major corporate boards within the United States. New CEO's have repeatedly been enlisted by Fortune corporations and guaranteed golden parachutes amounting to tens of millions of dollars, *regardless of performance.*

A notable case in point, Hewlett-Packard, has been plagued by recent CEOs changing the company's direction with alarming frequency. Results for the company, its employees, and stockholders have been disastrous, while sacked CEOs have repeatedly walked away unscathed and highly rewarded. Since 2007, HP's market valuation has nosedived 60% to only $35 billion. Meanwhile, during that same timeframe, HP's leadership has invested more than $40 billion on dubious acquisitions. Where is the ROI from these actions? Is it any wonder that following the past five years of repeated marketplace missteps, many investors have written-off HP as a viable marketplace contender going forward? To quote ISI Group analyst Brian Marshall, 'It has been a case of just horrible management.' In 2012, HP announced its plan to cut 29,000 employees across the company. HP CEO, Meg Whitman, said that layoffs would be spread out over the next two years through the end of fiscal year 2014 *in order to reduce the short-term harm to morale within the company.* Seriously? Will dragging out the inevitable, coupled with month after month of anxious employees wondering who will be fired next really preserve morale? Apparently, she is not concerned about long-term morale. Wonder why?

A common excuse among boards of directors maintains that such 'guaranteed' compensation packages, irrespective of actual performance, are necessary to attract top talent. Maybe it is time for these corporate boards to rethink the level of talent they need and are recruiting, given the appalling results being produced.

Whether in the executive suite or elsewhere across the organization, safety-blanket guarantees and risk-aversion are detrimental. If we truly desire new dimensions of performance, then we must be willing to accept risk, not as a millstone, but as a positive driver that will spur our organizations forward. My endorsement of risk may cause some readers to walk away from this book. But the truth is that effective innovation requires more than lip service — it can only be achieved by those willing to take the plunge and create truly innovative organizations — organizations wherein risk and reward are balanced and the commitment to innovation is real, beginning at the very top and permeating every layer, department and function. The CEO need not be the Chief Innovation Officer and in most instances, will not be, but he or she does need to assume the role of CIA: Chief Innovation Advocate.

Another misconception is that smaller companies cannot compete on the innovation playing field. Contrary to popular opinion, successful innovation has far more to do with attitude than the organization's size, amassed resources or even available funding. As Steve Jobs said, 'Innovation has nothing to do with how many R & D dollars you have. When Apple came up with the Mac, IBM was spending at least 100 times more on R & D. It's not about money. It's about the people you have, how you're led, and how much you get it.'

How fast can innovation turn even a large international company around? The Korean automaker Hyundai provides an excellent case study answer to this question. Jay Leno once joked that you could double a Hyundai's value by filling it up with gas, but no one in the auto industry is laughing today. With skyrocketing sales and three coveted North American Car of the Year Awards in just three years as well as being nominated for 2013 Truck of the Year, Hyundai, former maker of 'junk' automobiles, has become the fastest growing auto brand in the industry. How? Innovation. Innovation requiring risk.

According to John Krafcik, Hyundai's CEO of American operations, the first step was to upgrade product quality from the lowest in the industry and to become one of the best. Where is the risk in that you may ask? It came in the form of a decision to offer the industry's most extensive 10 year/100,000 mile power train warranty. According to Krafcik in an Associated Press interview, 'It was an absolute bet-the-company move. If we had gotten that one wrong, then the company would have failed. And rather quickly, too, as the warranty expense and exposure are significant when you're taking a bath that big.' Under Krafcik, Hyundai has pushed the envelope in many areas including design. At a time when other car makers are satisfied with producing cars that all look similar in each car category, Hyundai has broken out of the mold with one excitingly original design after another. 'It just takes courage and a willingness to take risks. So with Sonata, the conventional orthodoxy in the industry was midsize cars should be styled conservatively. This is typical market research talking...about number seven or eight on the (customer) pecking order is design. From that mentality has come the point of view that midsize cars should look like (Toyota) Camrys and (Honda) Accords and (Chevrolet) Malibus. Products starting with the '05 Tucson and the '06 Sonata were designed in a safe and conservative manner. It didn't move the needle in terms of sales. You go through that and you finally see the pattern. You can't just accept safe,' he states. Someone was willing to *put their neck on the block* to push forward an innovative idea, and it paid off. That someone was a Giraffe.

How many Giraffes do you need to make a miracle? For some organizations, one Giraffe is enough to drive innovation and change. Larger organizations require more, but no organization needs or would even thrive with a preponderance of Giraffes. They are like yeast: a little goes along way. Too much and the loaf is all air bubbles and no bread!

Nor do Giraffes need to be at the top of the organization. Often, they do fill the CEO spot in start-ups that emerge on the basis of new marketplace ideas or technologies. However, this can be damaging to an organization in instances where the Giraffe CEO who started the company lacks the managerial skills necessary to keep the organization growing and fails to realize it. It is important to understand that Giraffes can be effective at any level within an organization, provided they are equipped, empowered, and encouraged to undertake and promote innovation on an ongoing basis.

The vast majority of people within any organization are content with conventional methods and procedures. They appreciate consistent patterns and the comfort that predictable, routine operations provide. It is not that they are incapable of participating in — or even initiating — breakthrough innovation, it is simply that innovation does not enter the context of their perspective on daily activities. They are the 'good citizens' of the organization who keep things humming and the wheels turning smoothly. That is their primary contribution, ensuring consistency and reliability. Every organization needs a majority of these people.

While Giraffe innovators are vital to organizational growth, it is actually good that their numbers remain limited. They are the organizational anarchists! Unconcerned with consistency and reliability, their role is to create disruption. What makes them so determined to upset the applecart? Don't these miscreants realize this plays havoc with other people's lives? Perhaps, these renegades are only using innovation as an excuse to tear up the efforts of the 'good people' who work so hard to keep everything functioning smoothly?

No, of course not, but it may certainly seem so at times. Giraffe innovators are passionate individuals for whom achieving leap-ahead innovations will always take precedence over the ease of consistency and security. Although Giraffes are often magnetic, extremely likable personalities, they will become tenacious and resourceful to realize innovation. As wild-eyed visionaries, they are literally driven to act by the opportunities they see, but others cannot. At least, not at first. Steve Jobs foresaw the iPad thirty years before it became a reality. The idea never cooled. It was always percolating somewhere in the back of his mind.

Thomas Edison believed that, *'Discontent is the first necessity of progress.'* To accomplish the goal of breakthrough innovation, Giraffes recognize that existing paradigms must sometimes be blown-up in order to establish new ways of doing things. It is this need to facilitate creative destruction that gets Giraffes into trouble. Others who have settled into prevailing patterns of thinking and doing things, will lament the cost of the destruction because they cannot yet envision the benefits that will result. This is especially true when the structures being destroyed or challenged, happen to be of their own design.

Generally, 'ownership' is an excellent motivational principle. Unfortunately, sometimes the structures in which we hold ownership have become obsolete. 'Ownership' often calcifies into pride, compounding the existing inertia. In such cases, leadership may opt for keeping the peace and ditching proposed innovations.

Seasoned Giraffes have learned to anticipate the hesitancy and outright fear their actions may cause colleagues. They recognize the value of discretion, timing and a tactful approach. After all, if it is necessary to 'burn down the palace,' one needn't run around brandishing the torch!

Giraffe Example:

Mildred Hope Fisher Wood, PhD

It's a matter of matching the method to the child.

In 2011, at the age of 91, Mildred Hope Fisher Wood was inducted into The Iowa Commission on the Status of Women Hall of Fame for her many innovations in the field of special education.

When Wood began teaching in 1939, there was virtually no understanding of cognitive learning disabilities in children. Such children were categorized as immature, naughty, 'slow,' or mentally disabled. She 'considered her first year of teaching a failure.' That year, she instructed three sisters in a combined first and second grade class. One of the sisters had problems learning to read. Wood later discovered that the child suffered from impaired vision and hearing. 'I couldn't teach that child one thing that year,' Wood stated. That frustrating experience of failure motivated the young teacher to make a career shift to focus on children with learning disabilities and special education needs. This was a specialty field barely recognized by mainstream education at the time. 'I made up my mind I was going to learn to test and teach each and every child,' she remembered.

After teaching for a short while, Wood became a speech therapist and later served in higher education. Wood earned four degrees from the University of Northern Iowa, did postgraduate work at Syracuse University and the University of Oregon, and earned a doctorate at Indiana University. All of these academic pursuits were directed towards the study of learning disabilities in children and the development of new methodologies and instructional models for transforming children with special needs into competent learners.

Wood developed and taught the first learning disabilities courses offered by the University of Northern Iowa. She also facilitated hundreds of workshops for teachers, parents, principals, psychologists and juvenile court officers. As a pioneer in special education and learning disabilities, Wood's research has enabled hundreds of thousands of students to succeed academically and go on to lead productive lives. Her work was not only with children, but also involved mentoring and training their parents. Much of it consisted of creating a widespread awareness of the problem. Through years of tireless volunteering in communities and churches, she taught large numbers of people how to recognize and respond to learning disabilities.

For almost eight years, Wood wrote an advice column for parents and teachers, which was eventually compiled and published as an award winning book, *A Handful of Popcorn*, geared towards parents raising children with attention deficit hyperactivity disorder. She also co-authored a diagnostic test for identifying learning disabilities in preschoolers.

Wood was a founding member, board member, and president of the Iowa Learning Disabilities Association, and also a charter member of the National Association for Children with Learning Disabilities as well as a member of the National Learning Disabilities Board.

Chapter 2 — Thought Questions

1. Does our organization have at least one highly placed visionary?

2. Does the definition, ***Change that creates a new dimension of performance*** coincide with our view of innovation?

3. Does our organization value creativity above knowledge?

4. Does our organization see innovation as involving hard work, problem solving and risk?

5. What goes through our mind, when we read these statements?

   Innovation involves risk, it is not safe.

   If the majority, 80% or more, of their organization's Innovation initiatives do not fail, they are not really innovating — not stretching the envelope nearly far enough.

6. What is our organization's definition of innovation?

7. What is our organization's attitude toward balancing risk and reward?

8. Does the desire for on-going innovation permeate the leadership and management of every department and level of our organization?

9. What is our response to Thomas Edison's belief that, 'Discontent is the first necessity of progress?' How is discontent with the status quo treated in our organization?

10. Within our organization, has *ownership* become an obstacle to needed change?

11. What lessons can be applied to our work and organization from the life's work of Mildred Wood?

To Giraffes, limitations are merely transient – waiting to be dispelled by someone thinking through the puzzle.

Chapter Three: What Does a Giraffe Look Like?

No doubt about it, you can't miss a giraffe in nature! Their appearance is entirely unique: they are tall with long, graceful necks, attractively patterned coats in varying shades of brown against a buff colored background, large, lustrous eyes, substantial ears, horns, and tufted tails. 'Horns?' you may be wondering, 'Those are very odd-looking horns!' Giraffe horns are formed from ossified cartilage (cartilage that has become bone.) Thus, they are classified as ossicones. Some people fancy that they give the giraffe a wise or clever look, but that is a matter of opinion. On the other hoof, while human Giraffes may not be visually distinctive, but they still have a way of standing out.

Always thirsting for answers, Giraffes ask lots of questions. Discontented with a bland diet of established practices and paradigms, they have been known to 'kick' the status quo — making them instantly unpopular. And, as we know, some animals kick back.

An organizational Giraffe's appetite for solutions compels them, at times, to look elsewhere — outside of the organization and industry (open innovation), seeking fresh ways to tackle recurring problems. Given the chance, they reach for new ideas and better ways of doing things.

Interestingly, giraffes in the wild can also take things to 'new levels' in grasping for high leaves on acacia trees. Their long (typically 18-20 inches), dextrous, blue-black tongues are covered with hard growths called papillae which protect them from the acacia tree's vicious thorns. Human Giraffe innovators possess a similar agility and tenacity. They pursue innovations relentlessly despite obstacles, natural or man-made.

The giraffe's large eyes are set at the sides of its head affording a wide field of vision. This, along with their towering height, allows them to peer over obstacles and see not only the big picture, but far into the distance. Keenly aware of moving objects within its visual field, a giraffe is quickly alerted to danger.

Many organizational communities have been ambushed or suffered equally dire consequences for the lack of visionary Giraffes. Where were they? That's a very good question. Many have been driven into the 'outback' for taking unpopular stances or becoming a pest by persistently tugging at someone's sleeve to prompt action. In hostile terrain, many Giraffe innovators learn the art of camouflage. Hard knocks from voicing innovative and unwelcome ideas or persistently nudging peers toward 'outside-the-box' thinking will eventually cause them to give up or at least 'shut down.'

Some Giraffes end up relegated to the organizational 'bush.' Sure, they can *see* what's coming and may know the answer, but they aren't telling. In a culture where innovators are ostracized, it is likely that those Giraffes who remain will play it safe and 'blend.' In other words, they will concede to viewing the organization from the ground level only — like their peers.

It is important to understand the inner workings of a Giraffe innovator's mind. Their mental processes are really quite extraordinary. To begin with, they see the world through a very different lens. As I have already stated, they are constantly thinking about, if not articulating, the questions *'Why?'* and *'Why not?'* They tend to view circumstances as flexible, rather than fixed and permanent. To Giraffes, limitations are merely transient — waiting to be dispelled by someone thinking through the puzzle. They pursue answers relentlessly and from differing perspectives, until an approach is found which produces a breakthrough allowing the obstacle to be overcome.

Giraffes recognize that problems and dilemmas often contain the seeds of real opportunity. Instead of viewing problems as burdens, Giraffes perk up their ears and welcome challenges, exploring them to unlock otherwise invisible opportunities.

Another area in which a Giraffe's thinking differs is the way in which he or she perceives problems. People trying to resolve seemingly complex issues often look for complex solutions, but Giraffes instinctively understand that the best solutions are often surprisingly, even stunningly, simple.

For example, in the late 1950s, the soft drink company, 7 UP had a problem. Consumers were not satisfied that the soda had a zesty enough flavor. The typical solution would have been to begin tinkering with the formula, but Giraffe innovator Louis Cheskin had a far simpler and better idea. Altering the green color of the soda can by making it 15% more yellow, resulted in consumers responding in taste tests that the soda did, in fact, have the lemon-lime zing they desired. It is often true that our perceptions become our reality!

Typically, the organizational approach in seeking to resolve complex, or apparently complex problems is to load down the team assigned to it with extra resources, advice, and staff...which only serves to complicate matters. Giraffes recognize that frequently the real answer is to back away from the problem, with all its complexities, and look at the 'big picture.'

Recently, my son-in-law, Joel, was working on a very complex problem — part of the research for his PhD in Physics. The 'insurmountable' obstacle lay in the fact that there existed an almost infinite number of variables which could impact the outcome. He was not alone in his quest for a solution, as several large teams, including two at U.S. Government National Laboratories, were struggling with the same problem. The other teams were heavily funded, with substantial resources backing their effort. Joel was working with a small team and very limited funding. Yet, he achieved a startling scientific breakthrough, advancing the research greatly.

How? Was he that much smarter than everyone else working on the problem? As he is my son-in-law, I would like to think so, but his success is best explained by the fact that he approached the problem from a radically different perspective. The other teams attempted to isolate, identify, and resolve every possible variable. Joel's small research group chose instead to isolate only the most critical variables, those with the greatest known impact. This reduced the task to a mere fraction of the effort which would have been necessary using the conventional approach. Once this was done, he discovered that the other variables were effectively insignificant to the outcome. Result? Problem solved!

Giraffes understand that capitalizing on opportunities and finding optimal solutions to even the most convoluted problems often requires us to reduce the complexity in order to raise the problem-solving effort to a higher level. A macro systems view allows the apparent complexity to be reduced in order to identify the core issue(s).

Similarly, one of the dilemmas plaguing modern medicine is specialization into ever more isolated fields of study and practice due to the explosion of new medical knowledge and the inability of any single doctor to be proficient in every sub-practice. However, the danger here lies in a specialist's tendency to treat only that aspect of the patient's health represented by his or her particular practice specialty as discrete and unrelated to the whole. This is hardly a sensible approach.

Human bodies are not machines to be cured by isolating the correct 'fault code' and then fixing or replacing that distinct part in a manner disconnected from the whole. In contrast, the holistic philosophy of patient care views and treats the patient as a complete system or organism.

Likewise, in organizational life, every input will have an impact and a resulting output somewhere down the line and, far too often, it is not where or what we expected. Companies are organisms. They have identities, cultures, histories, traditions, etc.   When we desire to correctly view the problems and opportunities which form the catalysts for creativity, ideation, and subsequent innovation, we must do so with the full entity in mind: its structure and marketplace(s), as well as the broader global context in which we work and live. Today, few businesses exist purely on a local level, and even those that do can be suddenly derailed by changes on the world stage. Just look at what happens to businesses, local and international, each time gasoline prices spike at the pump and jet fuel and diesel skyrocket.

Giraffes have a unique ability to look at circumstances and events and see them in a far broader context than most people. This is not to imply that they are necessarily brighter than those around them, but rather that they are able to conceptualize innovation from a strategic, multi-dimensional viewpoint.

Most of us are familiar with paintings which, at first glance, project no more than an appealing woodland scene, a landscape of rocks and snow or other natural setting, but are, in fact, not as they appear. We are stunned by the sudden realization that hidden among the brown rocks and snow are ghostly figures of brown and white paint horses, Native American warriors along with other ingeniously disguised objects. As we adjust our perspective, the picture is transformed! We now realize that the painting we are viewing is actually two very distinct scenes, artfully integrated onto one canvas. Whichever scene your mind 'sees' at a given instant, creates an entirely different response.

This example illustrates the vast disparity between the way in which most people view opportunities and problems versus the multi-faceted perceptions of a Giraffe. Although the majority will see the picture and be able to identify its discrete elements, they cannot discern the relationship between those individual elements and a greater, hidden synergistic context. The manner in which Giraffes view the world is like the hidden images of horses and warriors versus the more obvious trees, rocks and snow depicted on the canvas. The Giraffe's perspective is visionary and strategic, encompassing *what is,* as well as *what could be,* in order to create a new reality. Giraffes lock onto the potential of what can be accomplished by achieving a solution which, in turn, may illuminate an otherwise obscure and inaccessible opportunity. Making that discovery their real goal, Giraffes reach for more than what may be discernible through a traditional, linear problem-solving approach. Again, they see above and beyond. They are visionaries.

Have you ever seen a Giraffe smile? That is what happens when they arrive at what is commonly referred to as an *idea*! Not only does the Giraffe's world light up, but the same is true for those around them who catch their vision. It is after all, contagious!

To feed the idea-making machine that runs incessantly inside their minds, Giraffes crave copious mental and visual stimulation. Frequently, what is going on in their heads is not directly related to what they may be doing at any given moment. Creative personalities live in two worlds: the world requiring their immediate attention and a subconscious realm of diverse images and ideas, capable of being summoned at any given moment. Not fully aware of these thoughts themselves, Giraffes have a reputation for appearing preoccupied.

Sometimes in the middle of important meetings, Steve Jobs of Apple would suddenly raise his hand in front of his face and turn it slowly, deeply immersed in thought — such an action might be perceived as 'disturbed' were it not the behavior of a known visionary such as Steve Jobs. But what was he doing? Jobs was amazed and intrigued by the design of the human body, especially the hand. At moments when he appeared to be lost in thought, looking at his hand, he was really using his mental processes to reset his thinking and return to the issues before him with a refreshed perspective.

Eighteenth century classical composer Wolfgang Amadeus Mozart is considered one of the greatest musical talents of all time, creating over 600 symphonic, concertante, chamber, operatic, and choral works. During his lifetime, Mozart was known to sit at the dinner table for hours at a time, quietly folding and refolding his dinner napkin. Meanwhile, his mind was actively generating the music he would later record on paper. He may have appeared to be doing nothing, but his genius was hard at work!

A Giraffe may be involved with the activities of a normal day when quite without warning, like a bolt of lightning, a random occurrence makes some sort of connection and the desired answer explodes into being. It could happen in a business meeting, while driving the car, eating a meal, or even in the middle of the night. In which case, the Giraffe may leap out of bed and quickly find a pen and paper to jot down the idea. (Most Giraffes have learned from experience that the thought may vanish just as quickly as it appeared.) Such are the creative processes of a Giraffe's mind, something which cannot be replicated by even the most advanced computers.

Ideas, inspiration, imagination, beauty – these are the things that excite Giraffes. When lightening strikes, a connection is suddenly made and the solution revealed, enabling the Giraffe to 'see' the potential innovation as though it already existed. It is as though a brilliant searchlight had been switched on and everything suddenly becomes crystal clear! A great idea is born and a breakthrough innovation begun. That is when a Giraffe smiles.

Giraffe Example:

George Washington Carver

When you do the common things in life in an uncommon way, you will command the attention of the world.

Although the exact date of his birth is unknown, George Washington Carver was born into slavery in Diamond, Missouri around 1864. A week after his birth, George was kidnapped from the Carver farm, along with his sister and mother, by raiders from the neighboring state of Arkansas. The family was transported to Kentucky and sold there. George was located by an agent of Moses Carver and returned to Missouri, but his sister and mother were never found.

After the Civil War, Moses and Susan Carver kept George and his brother James at their home, raising and educating the two boys as their own. Susan Carver taught George to read and write, since at that time, black students were not permitted to attend classes in the local schools. Later, after completing high school and stints at both Highland College in Kansas and Simpson College in Iowa, Carver enrolled in Botany at the Iowa State College of Agriculture and Mechanic Arts (now Iowa State University). He was the first black student to study at the university.

Carver proved an outstanding student and went on to earn a Master's Degree, performing extensive work in the study of plant pathology at the Iowa

Experiment Station. There Carver established a reputation as a brilliant botanist and commenced his life's work in botany.

In 1896, Booker T. Washington, then president of a small educational institute in Alabama called Tuskegee wrote to Carver asking him to head their Agriculture Department. 'Our students are poor, often starving,' Washington wrote. 'They travel miles of torn roads, across years of poverty. We teach them to read and write, but words cannot fill stomachs. They need to learn how to plant and harvest crops.' The letter closed with the following words: 'I cannot offer you money, position, or fame. The first two you have. The last, from the place you now occupy, you will no doubt achieve. These things I now ask you to give up.' In their place, Washington offered Professor Carver only hard work – the challenge of liberating people from poverty and degradation through education.

Carver decided to accept the offer. Upon arrival at Tuskegee, he found no laboratory for his plant research, but he had made a commitment. The students helped him to build a rough laboratory. Then they went to work restoring the nutrient content of an experimental twenty acre plot of land. First they grew cowpeas, then sweet potatoes, and finally cotton. The plot produced a bumper crop of a five hundred pound bale of cotton compared to the previous harvest of only two hundred pounds.

Carver set up a 'school on wheels' to bring new knowledge to farmers in the countryside. When the Boll Weevil infestation struck Alabama in 1914, Carver advised the farmers to plant something other than cotton. He suggested peanuts, as they are pod-bearing plants and grow underground. Unfortunately, the market became glutted with peanuts and the farmers found themselves in desperate financial straits because they could not sell all the peanuts. Carver prayed for a way to help the farmers. Countless experiments followed, by which he discovered nearly three hundred uses for peanuts. The products of this versatile plant included soap, cosmetics, dye, and ice cream. Carver also found creative uses for other crops, such as soybeans, pecans and at least one hundred fifteen uses for sweet potatoes. Carver only applied for and received three patents over the course of his lifetime, and he received no profit from the majority of his products. His products were developed for the benefit of humanity, he said, 'God gave them to me...How can I sell them to someone else?'

Under Carver's leadership, Tuskegee's Department of Agriculture became world renowned for innovative breakthroughs in farming techniques, products, and crop uses. He served as an agricultural advisor to Theodore Roosevelt during his presidency, as well as to Mahatma Gandhi of India. In 1916, Carver was made a member of the British Royal Society of Arts, quite an unusual honor for an American. Carver also advised on matters of agriculture and nutrition. He spoke frequently and was a strong advocate of innovation in agricultural methods.

In 1940, three years before his death, Carver donated his life savings to the establishment of the Carver Research Foundation at Tuskegee for continuing research in agriculture. He died in January 1943, at the age of seventy-eight and was buried next to Booker T. Washington at the Tuskegee Institute. His epitaph reads: 'He could have added fortune to fame, but caring for neither, he found happiness and honor in being helpful to the world.'

Each example of a Giraffe thus far begins with a quote that reflects that individual's perspective on innovation. However, in the case of George Washington Carver, the following four quotations are simply too priceless not to share.

Since new developments are the products of a creative mind, we must therefore stimulate and encourage that type of mind in every way possible.

There is no short cut to achievement. Life requires thorough preparation — veneer isn't worth anything.

Ninety-nine percent of the failures come from people who have the habit of making excuses.

Learn to do common things uncommonly well; we must always keep in mind that anything that helps fill the dinner pail is valuable.

Chapter 3 — Thought Questions

1. Does our organization have at least one Giraffe who frequently kicks the status quo?

2. If so, how do others normally respond?

3. Have I ever been part of an organization that was 'ambushed' by a competitor or marketplace disruption? If so, do I think having a visionary Giraffe on-board could have reduced or even prevented the negative repercussions?

4. Do we view problems as the seeds of potential opportunity? Could embracing a new view of innovation change our perspective?

5. What is our organization's approach to solving complex problems?

6. What thoughts does the 7 Up approach to solving their consumer taste test problem awaken in your mind? When approaching problems, does our organization consider the possibility that the best solution may not be the obvious one and that frequently the standard linear approach to analyzing problems and possible solutions misses the opportunity to act creatively?

7. When confronting potential opportunities and difficult problems, should the terms *why* and *why not, strategic, vision, what could be* and *possibilities* be applied in discussing what course of action should be taken?

8. Is there anyone in our organization who has come to be known, either formally or informally, as the 'idea person,' the 'go-to' person when fresh perspectives are needed?

9. Have I ever experienced an 'Aha' moment when the solution to an issue I had been struggling with suddenly became clear and laid out in my thoughts like a roadmap? If so, how did this make me feel?

10. What aspects of George Washington Carver's life demonstrate his persistently practical approach to innovation?

11. Do we think more breakthrough innovation would occur in our organization if everyone involved were less concerned with fire-fighting than creating something of value?

Organizational Giraffes can take their organizations very far, very fast by unleashing the power of innovation.

Chapter Four: What Can Giraffes Do For You?

Despite their very long necks, giraffes are unable to easily reach the ground when they need a drink. Fortunately, they are good problem solvers. By splaying their front legs, which are actually longer than their back legs, into a rather hilarious posture, they can touch the ground. This awkward position, however, creates a new problem. When they drink at the watering hole, they are vulnerable to attack by predators such as lions and crocodiles. The solution? Giraffes watch each other's backs, taking turns at the watering hole. Very strategic!

Giraffes are also the world's largest ruminant – meaning that they chew their cud. In a manner of speaking, human Giraffes also 'ruminate,' chewing over ideas and problems, revisiting a given issue and then turning it over again and again in their minds. Organizational Giraffes are strategic thinkers and problem solvers. Their exceptional *vision* allows them to peer over and around obstacles, and well into the distance foreseeing how future scenarios will unfold.

Giraffes create value first through *seeing* (recognizing) the opportunities where innovation may be employed to achieve new dimensions of performance and then by bringing those innovations into reality. Where do these great 'opportunities' exist? Clearly, innovation can be utilized to improve the results of virtually anything we undertake, but where will the payback be the greatest? The highest value opportunities exist wherever creativity can intersect with the highest value-added aspects of the business which varies by industry. For instance in high tech, innovation creates the biggest payback at the intersection of creativity and technology. In a people-intensive business, innovation is most profitable when applied at the intersection of creativity and the primary people interfaces.

To delve into this subject further, we can begin by looking at how Giraffes typically think about innovation. Let's review some things we have already considered. As visionaries:

1.   Giraffes think strategically.

2.   Giraffes see into the distance (future).

3.   Giraffes foresee developing trends.

4.   Giraffes recognize opportunities and problems.

5.   Giraffes visualize solutions.

Giraffe innovators have the ability to perceive where an organization is positioned today as well as what it has the potential to become tomorrow. When Giraffes are at the executive level within the organization, their focus will be the overall environment within which the company exists, including its products and services, customers and competitors, internal and external technologies, emerging markets, the worldwide geo-political stage, and a myriad of other factors. In other words, their view will be at the macro level.

When Giraffes function in an operational capacity, their focus will be on the organization, department or product group, as appropriate to their responsibilities, at a *micro* level. This does not by any means prevent a Giraffe from perceiving innovation on a much broader scale. However, in this scenario, their primary focus is not at the macro-level.

Furthermore, Giraffes typically view the world in terms of two distinct perspectives, which may initially seem worlds apart. That is, they think in terms of 'opportunities' and 'problems.' But from the Giraffe's point of view, these two seemingly polar extremes are, in fact, part of a dynamic continuum, as we will see shortly.

In regard to opportunity, we can note that Giraffes – especially those functioning at the macro organizational level – will view everything in terms of the broader world markets, which are always in a state of flux and hence opportunity. It is this state of constant change that creates many opportunities. Giraffes will always be asking, 'How can we position ourselves to maximize the developing opportunities we can identify from the trends we are watching?' To answer this question, Giraffes carefully examine:

1. The potential for new products and services.

2. The opportunity to reignite languishing or dying products and services.

3. The prospect of entering new markets.

4. Acquisitions and divestures.

5. Joint ventures, licensing and cross-marketing agreements.

6. Opportunities for changing internal functions including:

   - Customer Service

   - Processes

   - Methods

   - Procedures

   - Systems

   - Facilities

   - Corporate Culture

When tackling problems, the Giraffe constructs a mental framework for evaluating whether or not:

1. The organization may be headed into a dead end.

2. Current paradigms governing how the organization operates, both internally and externally, no longer match a rapidly changing marketplace reality.

3. More is at stake in solving a given problem than merely finding an acceptable solution.

All of the above fall within the scope of *what is today* versus *what can be tomorrow* and form the lens through which a Giraffe views the organization and the world.

In recent years, I have been disturbed by what I see as the push to solve problems too quickly. Not that a swift approach to solving major problems isn't important, but there is a growing tendency to seize upon any solution. It is as though the main goal were to simply cross it off a 'To Do List' and move on to the next item. Speed is important, but quality more so. In a hyper-competitive global world, we do not just need solutions. We need optimal solutions!

Sometimes 'triage' (prioritizing in terms of urgency) is necessary or the patient — in this case, the organization — may not survive, but that is the exception, not the rule. Generally, sufficient time exists to determine the optimal solution and implement it. The problem is with us. We are so pressured, time-pushed and exhausted from running around attending to the urgent, that opportunities to do what is truly important are often lost.

Yes, we may come up with a solution that solves the problem quite neatly, but the solution is short-term. And the problem only moved down the line to recur later, somewhere else. Perhaps you are familiar with the children's story about a kingdom that had a terrible problem. They were overrun with mice. In order to get rid of the mice, the king brought in cats, which created a bigger headache for his subjects than the mice. Then, to get rid of the cats, in came the dogs. It has been many years since I've read the book, but as I recall the problem kept getting bigger until they ended up with elephants, which could not be endured. So to get rid of the elephants, what did they do? They brought back the mice and learned to live with them. Sometimes no solution at all is far better than a bad one.

Rash solutions can be distressing, but even more so the fact that all too often no one asks whether there could be a silver lining, or maybe even a golden one, to the problem. Years ago, when I worked in the petroleum industry, an urgent request unexpectedly came in from Amoco Oil Company. Amoco was desperate – and when a major corporation is truly *desperate,* there is money to be made by whoever can solve the dilemma! At that time, Amoco had multiple U.S. refineries. A sudden decision had been made at the senior level of the organization, just prior to the end of winter, to permanently close their Sugar Creek refinery located in a suburb of Kansas City, MO. They had dealt with how to supply all of their commitments in that marketplace through the petroleum products pipelines and product exchanges with other suppliers with the notable exception of one. Asphalt. With the asphalt season imminent, they could not find another company with available supplies in the Kansas City marketplace and were beginning to think that their only recourse was to truck asphalt from their East Chicago, Indiana, refinery about 600 miles away.

This suggestion posed several major problems. Hot asphalt is loaded at the refinery at 300 °F or higher and must be delivered, depending upon the scale of the project, to either the asphalt plant or job site while it is still very hot. Otherwise, as the asphalt cools, it will harden into a solid block inside the truck. Should that occur, aside from burying the truck, there is only one solution: attach the tank trailer's internal heating coil system to a high pressure steam source and 'cook' the asphalt back up to molten temperature. This, however, is a slow and expensive process, since an industrial high-pressure boiler is needed to generate sufficient steam. The trailer and, in most cases, the tractor unit and driver are out of commission while this reheating occurs, burning up hundreds of dollars per hour per truck.

Secondly, the cost of trucking asphalt in a semi-trailer over six hundred miles is exorbitant. In fact, it is never advisable to truck asphalt more than a few hundred miles at most. Finally, the number of trucks Amoco would have needed to fulfill the contracts they had made at the end of the previous summer simply did not exist. Needless to say, the trucks needed for such a project are hardly standard tank trucks. They are insulated tankers fitted with high-pressure steam heating coils and, once used for asphalt, there is not much else they are fit to carry other than residual fuel oil, which is what refineries make in winter from the residue left from refining crude oil, in lieu of asphalt.

Now if you know anything about asphalt and refineries, you are already thinking, there must be a much more logical and less expensive solution. And you are absolutely right. Virtually all American refineries are located on railroad lines and, within the North American railroad system, there are tens of thousands of insulated, steam-coiled railroad tank cars that hold 23,000 gallons each, as opposed to the asphalt trailers that hold only 5,000 gallons each. So why not use those? The simple answer is that one must have a destination equipped to unload these jumbo tank cars into trailer trucks for delivery to the local asphalt plants. In all of the Kansas City area, the only place equipped to do so was none other than the Amoco Sugar Creek refinery that was in the process of being shuttered. This meant it no longer had the capacity to generate the steam needed to heat the railcars. Far more importantly, in order to unload anything there, it would be necessary to keep all of the refinery workers on the payroll. ALL? Yes, because the union contract specified that if even a single refinery function continued, all operations had to be fully staffed, whether operational or not. While I do not remember the exact numbers any more, it was not unusual to have at least 1,200 people working in that size refinery at that time. Refineries are, after all, 24/7/365 days per year operations.

So . . . Amoco was stuck. Our Director of Sales came to me and asked if I could 'think of a solution,' as even a company the size of Amoco was sweating the costs, and not about to default on their asphalt supply contracts.

I reviewed the situation and quickly decided that the only readily available supply of asphalt was that produced by Amoco in their East Chicago refinery. Secondly, the only reasonable way to move it the six hundred miles was by railcar. Truck and barge were out of the question in this circumstance and you cannot move asphalt in a pipeline. The only remaining problems were where to unload in the Kansas City area and how to be ready to begin large scale operations within little more than a month.

I could clearly visualize the solution. We would unload the railcars into trucks in an existing railroad yard. All we needed to do was to create a complete, scalable, mobile asphalt transfer station that could be speedily set-up and dismantled in the midst of an extremely busy railroad yard in the middle of Kansas City. *No problem!* Although it did pose a few associated minor issues, which included:

1.   Railroads do not like other people playing in their railroad yards, especially one of their largest primary yards. To begin with, these are dangerous places. Injuries and fatalities can occur, particularly at night and in inclement weather. It is amazing how quiet a slow moving freight train can be and how, on a dark night, it can appear suddenly – out of nowhere.

2.   There are huge liability issues, both legal and with OSHA, when someone is injured or dies, especially a non-railroad employee.

3.   At that time, all major railroads were unionized. However, our crew was expressly non-union, as were many of the truckers the asphalt companies would be using, which created a work rules complication.

4.   Most railroad yards are not equipped with a source of steam, at least not of the type and capacity we needed.

5.   Unloading asphalt requires heavy, high-pressure hoses; massive, high-volume positive displacement pumps; and lots of electrical power to run them, not to mention the steam generator, insulated steam lines, etc.

6.   Operating any type of bulk liquids terminal carries with it the near certainty of spills, at least small ones. Petroleum spills invariably pollute the soil and require containment and environmental clean-up.

7.   Asphalt is sold by the ton, not the gallon, so a state inspector certified portable truck scale would be required. These in themselves are minor feats of electronic and structural engineering requiring special ground preparations and insulation from vibration, not easy when hundred car freight trains are constantly rumbling past just a few yards away. Such scales have a large footprint, ten feet wide by seventy feet long, plus requiring ramps that add an additional twenty-five feet in length on each end.

8.   Ingress and egress for up to a hundred or more semi-tractor trailers per 24 hour period, which would be driving across active railroad tracks, not protected by signals, carrying 5,000 gallon loads of combustible petroleum.

9.   The safety, fire-fighting, document processing and other equipment as well as a full infrastructure for the 24/7 workers at least six days a week, rain or shine.

10. And there was one final issue, at first overlooked in the excitement of *seeing* the golden opportunity hidden within this problem. This occurred in a day when railroads were one of the most heavily regulated industries in America. As there had always been refineries in both Kansas City and the Chicago area, no one had ever shipped asphalt by railroad between the two cities. Consequently, there were no existing published rail tariff rates.

In those days, negotiating and obtaining quick approval and publication of a new railroad tariff rate took four to six months. We had just over a month to be operational.

All this was to take place in a busy railroad switch yard where trains are arriving, being broken down, sorted, reconfigured and then built into new trains every hour of the day and night. But other than those few snags, life was good, very good indeed! I knew I was on a roll to do just what the Chairman and President of the company I worked for had tasked me with— finding our future by expanding our products and services into new markets.

What then? I told the Amoco executives that I needed committed numbers based on making it happen at costs they could live with – without telling them how. It was one of those 'just trust me' moments in business, when your client simply stares at you with a dazed expression, trying to determine whether they have just committed their future to a savior or a lunatic.

After a day of frantic phone calls from Amoco, I had the committed volumes from which I could project revenues and expenses. I pulled in my engineering 'team' of one – a very bright guy with a perfect record for bringing in every cost projection *amazingly* below the ultimate actual cost. I was always in a quandary with the numbers he gave me. *Should I multiply them by two or is three a more realistic cost estimate?* But to his credit, he built everything he committed to, usually in record time and often under very unfavorable conditions. It simply cost more! Frequently much more!

Next stop were the railroads and, fortunately with a Chicago - Kansas City run, I had several railroad choices from which to generate healthy competition. Armed with the numbers from Amoco, I had immediate access to salivating senior executives at each railroad company. Each time I began with the good news: the tonnage. And what a tonnage it was! It would be six fabulous months of new traffic – a winner take-all deal. No dividing this one up. Every railroad I spoke with was ready and willing to deal on tariff rates and quickly.

Then came the catch. I needed a $1 lease of two very long (2,000') side by side tracks inside their main railroad yard where we could erect and operate a non-union, mobile terminal facility (aka The Terminal-On-Wheels) to unload the asphalt into semi-trucks.

At first, the responses were incredulous. *You want to do what? Where? No, not possible. Not in a million years! Certainly not in the month or less that you require.* I'll skip over the negotiations, but within less than a week, the Santa Fe railroad was on board and we were in their main Kansas City yard prepping the ground.

Not only did Amoco meet all of their commitments for asphalt in the Kansas City market that summer, but as we proved our capabilities, Amoco began increasing their asphalt sales each month at the expense of their competitors. They extended our contract further into the autumn in order to maximize sales. More importantly, by the end of the season we were already under contract to do it again the next summer. This little, 'Could I think of a solution?' effort had turned into a nice seven-figure piece of profit and that, after all of the investment had already been amortized 100%.

Then we took the next step and began marketing the Terminal-On-Wheels concept for other difficult to handle, liquid, bulk product requirements, both leasing and selling scalable mobile terminal units. When you approach problems with more than just a 'How do we solve this problem as quickly as possible?' mindset, you may uncover some of your greatest opportunities.

In hot pursuit of solutions, Giraffes are relentless. When they encounter a barrier, they will typically convert it into a mental image. By so doing, they can visualize it fully, turning it over again and again in their minds, ruminating consciously and unconsciously over it, until the solution is found. Although it is truly an innate capacity, this ability can be sharpened and perfected with regular use and experience. Experienced Giraffes who have been actively solving problems for many years have keener perceptions. They are quick to identify the highest impact opportunities and solutions for optimal breakthrough results.

But Giraffes can do more than spot strategic opportunities and solve complex problems. Organizations have much to benefit from having a Giraffe on the C-level executive team by adding the position of Chief Innovation Officer (CIO). This executive role should spearhead the development and implementation of market-changing innovations. In the contemporary marketplace, success depends only partially on the mechanics of getting products and services to market. In most instances, that has become the easy part of business. The means for accomplishing, systematizing, and managing those tasks are well established and readily executed in virtually any marketplace and organization. Today, the difference between success and failure, remaining relevant or not, hinges on the steady and continuous flow of breakthrough innovative ideas for gaining and maintaining a competitive edge, rather than merely achieving efficiency in daily operations. By saying this, I am not by any means inferring that operational excellence is not critical, but rather that the solutions for doing so are readily at hand and have been thoroughly proven and documented across most industries. However, the culture and continuous pursuit of open innovation is, in most organizations, still in its infancy.

In today's economy, organizations compete in one of two ways:

1. *Price*. The lowest price on the street will always have takers. However, over time customers realize that the company with the lowest prices is either dying a slow death or in the risky business of buying time through ever deeper cost savings. This is accomplished by reducing product quality, customer service and warranties or by scrimping elsewhere. When the price keeps falling, the value the customer receives cannot remain constant forever. The only exception to this rule is where a company achieves ever greater economies of scale, allowing perpetual cost savings. For most industries, such economies of scale were wrung out of the equation long ago.

2. *Innovation.*   The second and more productive competitive strategy is to discover a way to reposition your firm as a marketplace leader by achieving advantage in design, technology, service, warranties or any number of aspects within one or more industries or marketplaces as demonstrated by the Hyundai example in Chapter Two.

Given the alternatives, the first – buying market share, then struggling to hold onto it – amounts to an ill-fated long-term strategy. Unless of course, the company has a very unusual way of controlling its costs which its competitors cannot match. Such industries do exist, but they are very rare.

In a shrinking, globally interconnected world, the only way to build a secure future (apart from possessing a unilateral advantage) is to create one or more unique propositions for achieving a sustainable competitive advantage — propositions that are capable of being strategically, not merely tactically, developed — going forward. This is where Giraffes can play a vital role within the organization. While they will likely be the primary discoverers of high Return on Investment (ROI) innovations, they can also enlist the help of others in developing those innovations, cultivating creativity at every level throughout the organization.

Breakthrough innovation can and should be simultaneously occurring everywhere within the organization, not just among a select few. The Giraffes may lead, but they cannot be the only players tasked with innovation in an organization that stakes its future on gaining and maintaining a strategic edge.

For the organization as a whole to be transformed into a hotbed of innovation, creative ideation must be encouraged and supported by an approachable leadership. Pooling collective experience and institutional knowledge, engaging in dialog and inquiry, abandoning established thinking patterns – all of these being essential components of successful innovation.

Giraffes challenge others to stretch their creative muscles by stepping outside of, even leaping over, existing paradigms. Giraffes are the Steve Jobs' and the Steve Wozniak's of the world. Given the opportunity, resources and – most importantly – encouragement, Giraffes can become virtual wellsprings of ideation, inspiring others to follow their lead. The more they overflow with spectacular innovations, the faster and more widely the organization catches the vision.

Innovation is *viral.* It spreads from one person to the next. Every organization needs innovation 'virus carriers' and the more Giraffes rub shoulders with others, the faster innovation spreads. *Giraffe thought leaders ignite the dynamic of synergistic collaboration.*

While Giraffes may not see it as their 'calling' to produce other Giraffes, they do love watching others 'catch the bug' and become suddenly aware that hidden within them is the capacity to partake in the process of innovating. Most people find it intensely satisfying to participate in significant innovation. Becoming a valued contributor reinforces a sense of community and self-worth.

The most effective Giraffes are people motivators encouraging those around them to think more creatively and to collaborate more openly and effectively. Wise Giraffes have learned to demonstrate patience with others and take the time to listen to their input. Colleagues who may be less creative, but who are more detail oriented, will be likely to catch crucial points that may have been missed. This is the benefit of teamwork.

While each participant is challenged to develop their unique capacities to the fullest, they must also level the organizational playing field by learning to function as a team – openly sharing, discussing, and examining ideas – pooling their skills and collectively devising ways to implement the best ideas quickly. To do so, they must shift from seeing themselves as separate and territorial to becoming part of a shared vision, a common goal.

This creates the dynamic of collaborative synergy. Synergy occurs when the whole exceeds the sum of the parts. Giraffes radiate a passion and creative energy which excites and inspires co-workers to embrace a vision and push beyond all limitations to achieve 'BIG BANG' synergistic outcomes.

After all, the power of innovation is indisputable. Historically, innovations have created or altered entire industries and changed the political/military balance of the world. In 1888, at the age of twenty-five, farm boy-innovator Henry Ford, found work maintaining steam engines as an engineer at the Edison Illuminating Company. Within five years, he rose to the position of Chief Engineer. Thomas Edison recognized the young man's remarkable gifts and encouraged him in his vision to build an automobile. Henry Ford named his first model The Ford Quadricycle. In 1903, he established Ford Motor Company, but this was only the conduit for his most famous innovation — the manufacturing assembly line. He had the idea of making cars affordable for families. As a result, Ford designed and developed the first assembly line for the mass production of automobiles.

The Model T, introduced in 1908, had a twenty horsepower, four-cylinder engine with a top speed of forty-five miles an hour. This ushered in a new era of transportation for Americans. One innovation would lead to another as continuous developments were made to the comfort and efficiency of the automobile. The first automobiles were black, but that would change. In 1927, the sleeker Model A, available in nine body styles and three colors (grey, green and black) replaced the traditional Model T. The improved version included innovations such as: a safety glass windshield, shock absorbers for comfort, wheel brakes, and a forty horsepower engine. And this was only the beginning...

Apparently, Henry Ford was not the first to *think up* an assembly line. By peering beneath the patina of hollow-cast Greek and Roman statues, leading authorities on classical bronze sculpture have now determined that these so-called masterpieces were copies, mass produced to keep up with the high demand for villa ornaments. Henry Lie, a curator and the director of Harvard

University's Strauss Center for Conservation and Technical Studies, stated that the ancient bronze foundry 'was a production line, a business arrangement.' This was made possible due to the technological breakthrough of lost-wax casting.

Fast-forward to Venice in the 1100s. At that time, the Venetian Republic Arsenal was Europe's first great military/industrial complex, encompassing over one hundred acres (about fifteen percent of the land area of Venice at the time) and incorporating both production and repair shipyards. Utilizing a basic form of assembly-line production and employing as many as three thousand skilled workers and laborers at its peak, the Arsenal could produce and launch up to two warships per day. Together with the city's strategic trade treaties, the Arsenal enabled Venice to become the naval superpower, which would dominate much of the Mediterranean from the early 1100s until the fall of the Venetian Republic to Napoleon in 1797.

Innovation will always trump 'lean' and other incremental management techniques in attaining sustainability. The Model T proved phenomenally successful. But what if the Ford Motor Company had decided to back burner innovation and just ride out the wave? Profits would have continued to climb and expenses would have declined . . . for a while. Although *lean* can serve an important short term tactic, it becomes dangerous when companies succumb to the temptation of making it a long term strategy, as the resulting 'anti-cost' mindset can become entrenched, produce inertia and undermine the innovation paradigm. With Ford, progress would have ground to a halt and who knows how long cars might have remained just plain black? Automakers today could utilize lean and save untold millions annually, if they would just paint all cars black. Or, why not take it a step further, and leave the new cars 'buck naked' with only the gray primer undercoat. Yes, cost effective, but no, not a good marketing strategy.

There is a reason everyone purchases shiny, new cars, or at least wants to do so. Stylish, brightly-colored cars stir the emotions and stimulate the imagination.

If I buy that shiny, new sports car with a capability of 140 mph and speed-rated summer compound tires (despite the fact that I live in Wisconsin where winter storms can bury the pavement with 100+ inches of snow annually and the thermometer can plummet to −30°F), for one sweet moment, on a bright summer day, I too can experience the rush of excitement and pure joy of driving *Mario Andretti* style. That's marketing! And it is marketing innovations that sell cars!

In the wild, giraffes have a distinctive walking gait, moving both right legs forward, then both left legs forward. At a gallop, the giraffe simultaneously swings its hind legs ahead of and outside of its front legs approaching speeds of thirty-five miles an hour, which is pretty fast!.

Organizational Giraffes can take their organizations very far, very fast by unleashing the power of innovation. They are visionaries, proficient problem solvers, and natural ideators. At the moment of opportunity, a Giraffe's goal is to initiate, develop, and implement game-changing innovation. Innovation that can and should become viral throughout every organization.

When given the opportunity, Giraffes can change your organizational paradigms. They inspire active involvement in the ideation process. They 'infect' the workplace with a robust dynamic in which creativity and teamwork thrive. They strive to continually implement market-changing innovations. Through their efforts, you will be able to outpace your competition.

Giraffe Example:

Carroll Shelby

I'm not particularly good at anything. I just like to bring people with great talents together and see what happens.

Carroll Shelby, a Texas chicken farmer turned hot-rodder and then professional auto racer, went on to build innovative sports cars like the Cobra that for the first time challenged Europe's longtime dominance of high performance sports car production and road racing. Shelby also designed high-performance versions of production cars like the Dodge Viper and Ford Mustang.

Shelby was an American race car driver, automotive designer, and entrepreneur. He was best known for his racing feats and for creating the Shelby American Cobra, and later developing the Mustang-based performance cars known as Mustang Cobras for Ford Motor Company. Founded in 1962, Shelby American Inc. continues to provide modified Ford vehicles, as well as high performance parts. Shelby Cobra sports cars have proved worthy competitors to Ferrari, Maserati, and Jaguar. Today the original Shelby Cobras are prized collector's items, commanding six and seven-figure prices at auction.

Innovation was a key to Shelby's success in the car racing industry. Bill Neale, an automotive artist who illustrated Shelby's designs, once recalled for an article in *Vanity Fair* that, when Shelby assembled his first Cobra, he painted it yellow and had it photographed for the cover of a magazine. The next day, he showed another magazine a second seemingly identical car, painted bright red. 'I said, 'You have two of them?' Neale recalled. 'And he [Shelby] said, 'Nah, we just painted it so they think we have two." Shelby promoted his Cobra by offering test drives to the automotive press and continued his practice of repainting the same car a different color each time a different magazine staff test drove it, giving the appearance of many cars in production.

In the early 1950s, Shelby began competing as a race car driver, driving various cars including a hot rod Ford fitted with a flathead engine. In May 1952, he drove in his first road race behind the wheel of an MG-TC, taking first place in a competition with other MGs. That same day, against hotter competition from Jaguar XK 120s, he won again. By January 1954, Shelby had attracted the attention of Aston Martin Team Manager John Wyer and met international Grand Prix driving greats Juan Fangio and Peter Collins. On the strengths of Shelby's racing expertise behind the wheel of a Cad-Allard, Wyer invited Shelby to co-drive an Aston-Martin DB3 at Sebring racetrack in Florida.

In March 1955, although Shelby was still undergoing operations to recover from a severe racing accident, he continued to race with his arm in a specially made fiberglass cast and his hand taped to the steering wheel. At Sebring, Shelby drove a 3.0-liter Monza Ferrari with Phil Hill. By then Shelby's career as a race car driver was really beginning to take off. In both 1956 and 1959, *Sports Illustrated* magazine named Shelby, 'Driver of the Year.' In June 1959, co-driving an Aston Martin DBR1/300, Shelby won the 24 Hours of LeMans.

Shelby competed in his last race in December 1960 and won the USAC driving championship for 1960. Two years later, in March 1962, Shelby-

American began operations. In April, the first Cobra CSX 2000, was painted pearlescent yellow and shipped to the New York Auto Show for the Ford display. Dealers began ordering and Shelby-American committed to building its new Cobra CSX 2000. In December 1963, the Cobra won the United States Road Racing Championship. In March 1964, Shelby-American entered a 427 cubic inch engined Cobra, CSX 2166, at Sebring in the prototype class. For the first time ever, Cobras beat Ferrari GTOs. In June 1964, Cobras won the GT class at the 24 Hours of Le Mans, defeating Ferrari. The Cobra finished fourth overall and first in the GT class. In November 1964, the 427 Cobra production prototypes were completed. Meanwhile, the 289 Cobra again won the SCCA A-production national championship.

In June 1966, Ford and Shelby American made history as GT-40 Mark IIs crossed the finish line at Le Mans 1-2-3, marking the first time an American team had won at Le Mans. In June 1967, Ford won at the 35th running of Le Mans with the GT-40, which was driven by A.J. Foyt and Dan Gurney under Shelby's direction (he was now the team owner). In 1968, one of Shelby's GT-40s took first place at Le Mans once again.

In June 1990, at age 67, Shelby received a heart transplant. A year later, he started the Carroll Shelby Heart Fund to help finance organ transplants for children in need. The foundation has the following aims:

- Helps children to combat life-threatening illnesses.

- Supports a variety of organizations dedicated to providing medical assistance.

- Funds scholarships in the field of automotive education.

- Supports educational programs in automotive and related fields.

In October 1992, Shelby was inducted into the International Motor Sports Hall of Fame. And, at age 80, Ford Motor Company once more called upon Shelby to assist in designing the most recent version of the Shelby Mustang.

Carroll Shelby's career is often described as that of a promoter, but at heart he was a consummate Giraffe, with a unique ability for product vision and innovation which was recognized by companies such as Aston Martin, Chrysler and Ford Motor Company. Through his vision of what 'could be' versus what 'was,' his innovations forever altered the future of the American sports car.

Chapter 4 — Thought Questions

1. Where will the highest value innovation opportunities likely be found within our organization?

2. Where else can significant innovation opportunities be found?

3. What characteristics differentiate Giraffe innovators from others?

4. Why isn't just finding solutions to problems good enough?

5. In our organization, what characteristics distinguish a macro versus a micro viewpoint of innovation?

6. What paradigms may be obsolete and frustrating our organization's ability to create breakthrough innovations?

7. Are the Giraffes within our organization actively influencing those around them to become more innovative?

8. Does our organization have a Chief Innovation Officer (CIO) on the 'C'- level team?

9. What is our organization's primary competitive advantage? Can it provide future sustainability?

10. Does our organization evidence the dynamic of collaborative synergy?

11. Is our organization 'infected' by a robust environment in which creativity and teamwork thrive?

12. What lessons can we learn from Carroll Shelby's career?

Organizations eager to realize the benefits of innovation must create an innovation-friendly environment for their Giraffes.

Chapter Five: What Do Giraffes Need to Prosper?

Good people are hard to come by and even harder to keep. Giraffes are essential to creating a culture of innovation, the lifeline to an organization's future. So how do you keep a Giraffe happy? It takes some doing. The care and feeding of Giraffes is no small undertaking. They need encouragement, appreciation, regular support and definitely a well-placed 'someone' within the organization to watch their backs.

While in some organizations protecting the Giraffe(s) is seen as a priority, in many others, it is not. The reason for this oversight lies in the fact that many executives lack a clear understanding of the immense contribution Giraffes can make to the bottom line. However, it is imperative that executive leaders connect with their Giraffes in the process of creating innovation. Leadership must empower them by providing the internal support they need to develop the breakthrough innovations needed to keep your organization on top.

As new ideas tend to 'upset the applecart,' Giraffes can be easily misunderstood. People generally resist change, even when it is much needed and long overdue. Because innovation usually requires internal change, Giraffes have a way of getting under their co-workers' skin. In the midst of a project, Giraffes may be so intensely preoccupied with the 'goal' that they are often completely unaware of trouble brewing. It is in precisely these situations that they are most vulnerable to attack. As I have stated before, when radical measures are required co-workers may become defensive and territorial. Your unsuspecting 'big picture' Giraffe might be ambushed or, at the very least, beset with snarls and swipes as well as delaying tactics. That is why, in supporting Giraffes, it is crucial that leadership stands behind their efforts, in other words, watches their backs.

Organizations eager to realize the benefits of innovation must create an innovation-friendly environment for their Giraffes. When a Giraffe *sees* a juicy market opportunity, leadership must recognize the need to respond promptly. It is true that Giraffes, at these times, can try one's patience. When they see an opportunity, they are driven to act and quickly, before that door of opportunity closes or a competitor snatches it away. Consequently, Giraffe innovators will be frustrated by months or even weeks of deliberating. This is when they require an advocate, someone who will expedite or temporarily circumvent the traditional and often needlessly bureaucratic 'planning and preparation' phase.

In a globally competitive marketplace, timing is crucial. In the vast majority of instances, real opportunities will vanish nearly as quickly as they appear. Giraffes realize that time is rarely on the side of innovation, so they 'push hard' for action, sometimes very hard, which can ruffle the feathers of those who neither *see* the opportunity clearly nor fully sense its urgency.

Another source of contention may be found in the fact that Giraffes *see* the opportunities for innovation with perfect clarity, when frequently it is not at all obvious to others. This visual clarity brings with it the imperative for action. With a clear, unobstructed view, Giraffes will see things distinctly and in sharp contrast. Those around them may prefer more time to research and consider alternatives, which often degenerates into *analysis paralysis* and exasperates the Giraffes because they see 'Rome burning' and want to act.

Giraffes can not only *see* the ultimate outcome, often they can simultaneously *visualize* the roadmap of steps and processes entailed, from start to finish. While their peers may still be trying to grasp the overview, the Giraffe has already solved the puzzle with the picture in their mind complete

— all of the actions and major steps foreseen. In fact, so much clarity at once can amount to a sensory overload leaving others more than a little confused. Even though it ultimately makes sense, the immediate bewilderment may lead to hostility – a *Let's just shoot the messenger and make life easier,* reaction.

The Giraffe's *visualizing* may sound mystical, but it is not at all uncommon in the process of creative ideation. Take, for instance, the example of James Watts, the Scotsman who invented the first rotary-motion steam engine in 1781, the innovative discovery which powered the Industrial Revolution. Watts had been wrestling with the problem for more than a year when on a particularly fine afternoon in 1765, he set out for a walk. 'I was thinking upon the engine at the time,' he wrote later, when – as he walked past the old washing house – 'an idea came into my mind that as steam was an elastic body it would rush into a vacuum, and if a communication were made between the cylinder and an exhausted vessel it would rush into it, and might there be condensed without cooling the cylinder....I had not walked farther than the golf-house (this was Scotland, mind you) when the whole thing was arranged in my mind.'

Giraffes can be challenging in other ways. Where most people strive to create stability and preserve the status quo, Giraffes would rather wipe the slate clean and start all over in order to see a more viable and beneficial alternative take its place. They are not afraid to employ creative destruction where necessary. However, this statement does not imply that they are wanton destroyers. Giraffes simply want to see their ideas realized for the good of the entire organization as well as its customers – and to that end they are driven.

In what other ways can an organization's leadership nurture and support these gifted individuals? Wild giraffes live in Africa's savannas and tree-dotted grasslands. They are happiest where they can roam freely. What Giraffe innovators need most in the 'organizational jungle' is space. Space to think, discover, and ideate— to move about freely and feed the imagination.

Organizational Giraffes do not appreciate being in confined quarters, aka the organizational cubicle. Naturally, they gravitate towards windows. Giraffes need to be *let out* on a frequent basis, as their inner world revolves around ideas, and ideas require a constant diet of experiences, visual stimuli, and intellectual nourishment to flourish. In the wild, giraffes consume up to one-hundred-forty pounds of food a day (surpassed in quantity only by the elephant.) In fact, they have been called the ultimate browsers. Although a giraffe's menu consists mostly of acacia leaves, they will dine on close to a hundred different trees. They enjoy munching on a diverse assortment of flowers, shrubs, trees, and (during droughts) even evergreens. Interestingly, they do not usually overgraze the land but instead stimulate the plants to produce new shoots. In nature, giraffes spend up to 75% of their day eating and then ruminating, chewing it all over again.

'Variety is the spice of life,' and your Giraffes need bucketfuls to satisfy their thirst for ideas. In business, that nourishment may come in many forms. It may be found in formal discussions and planned meetings to consider the organization's strategic outlook, but also informally among employees eager to share ideas and intelligence regarding new developments. Steve Jobs considered innovation 'a group activity' involving cross-functional collaboration. As creative personalities, organizational Giraffes will not thrive in highly structured environments because they limit the possibilities. Moreover, formal meetings with strict agendas are not likely to supply the mental sustenance necessary for innovation. All too often, what is intentionally left off the meeting agenda for internal political reasons may reflect the most critical issues facing an organization. Hot button topics often mask the very issues offering the greatest opportunities for innovation.

A Giraffe's appetite for visual stimuli must be fed frequently and in large doses. Color, pattern, texture, theme, and design all provide vitally important stimuli. Nothing kills the output of a creative mind faster than boredom. If your office appears lifeless and drab, then take another look. Where is there room for improvement? Consider the offices of companies in industries where breakthrough innovation occurs regularly, for instance in the high tech industry, Apple and Google, or in another market, Zappos. It is no coincidence that their offices are anything but bland and dull. On the contrary, they are wildly novel — pulsating with vibrant colors and design motifs. Though typically more function than fancy, they still get high marks for creativity.

I cannot emphasize enough the fact that Giraffes are not comfortable with highly defined structures or a high degree of regimentation. They are your in-house innovation *artists*. While they may not use palate and brush, they are exceptionally creative personalities. However, the *art* they create is purpose driven.

There is significant confusion within executive leadership ranks as to what a Giraffe produces. An artist creates a work of art, which is an end in itself. Similarly, those tasked with innovation all too frequently see the creative process or the creating of *something new* to be an end in itself. But innovation is not merely a matter of creating something new. Innovation is the act of creating something with purpose and the proof of that purpose is actualized in terms of bringing new value to the organization. A product without a marketplace or a customer who wants it and is willing to pay for it is not *purpose*. A change in how the company is organized or operates that does not create new efficiencies, effectiveness or cost savings is not *purpose*.

A creative person within your organization is not a Giraffe innovator unless their output results in *'Change that creates a new dimension of performance.'* I have witnessed many innovation efforts that failed miserably, because the bright, hard working people involved were highly creative, but not driven by the needs of the marketplace. They were artists, creating something that had value to them alone.

Giraffe innovators are a different kind of artist. They too are highly creative individuals, but they are also driven relentlessly by a burning passion to see their innovations become reality, a reality that makes a positive difference. I term this passion 'focused creativity,' for it is creativity applied effectively to real world opportunities and problems.

Just as you will not find artists flocking to highly-structured environments, neither are Giraffe innovators suited to being *fenced in*. They need flexible schedules in order to investigate high value opportunities for creating innovation. Opportunities are unpredictable and will not necessarily follow a linear path, where step A, leads to step B which in turn leads to step C and so forth. Like an exploding nova, ideas have a way of bursting into existence when and where they are least expected.

The implementation of an innovation will often need to cut across departmental and organizational lines. Particularly in the investigation, planning and roll-out phases, traditional hierarchies can impede and even halt that progress. Innovators need to be afforded effective means of overcoming such barriers. As I have already mentioned, time is the enemy of innovation. When opportunities arise for breakthroughs or solving problems through innovation, speed is critical. The archenemies of innovation are 'Not Invented Here' and 'Death by Committee.'

Each day the race for competitive advantage begins anew. While innovators chafe at the bit, their worst fears come to pass when 'paralysis by analysis,' large committees and long chains of approval, doom their innovations. For innovation to thrive, Giraffes must believe their efforts will not end in futility. Fast-track methods must be devised for expediting initiatives as quickly as opportunities unfold. The saying, 'Haste makes waste' may be true, but who can deny that in business, 'Time and tide wait for no one'? For innovation to succeed, the goal is not haste, but speed. Speed is the result of swift, decisive and effective action.

Leadership must also provide clear direction and accountability for continuous innovation to be successful. This means neither the dreaded extreme of micro-management nor a bird's-eye view oversight from the executive suite, but rather, it implies a hands-on involvement in setting standards of performance and ensuring that those standards are not allowed to slip.

Sacrificing 'what can be' for what is considered possible, all too frequently becomes the fallback position. As a result, innovations originally envisioned as breakthrough, end up being incremental at best. Returning for a moment to the Apple business model, when Steve Jobs demanded that the original mouse and first iPhone have only one button, or that the iMac run silently without the incessant whirring of a fan motor, the engineering teams said it could not be done. At one design review after another, they came back with the same answer, 'not possible.' Yet, Jobs kept sending them back to the lab with his unflinching mandate, ' Find a way!' Was he just that stubborn? No! Intent on creating the ideal product, he would accept nothing less.

Teams developing innovation at the detail level need the freedom to discover the best way to make it happen. At the same time, leadership must ensure that downgrades do not occur in the ultimate design and performance parameters.

At one time, my consulting firm managed the U.S. office and operations of a European client that was developing a new $350,000 industrial instrument for analyzing gas well charts. When the long overdue device was completed, we were notified that the validation testing had been successfully conducted in Europe. Units which had already been pre-sold in the U.S. were then shipped directly to customers. When the units arrived, a high percentage of inaccurate results rendered them unusable, due to the wide variation of types, styles and colors of gas charts resulting from tens of thousands of individual gas well recorders.

As the units had already been placed in service with multiple major U.S. oil and gas companies when these deficiencies became apparent, a solution to the problem and an immediately workable field 'fix' was imperative. During the R&D stage, the company had utilized the technical expertise of a highly respected European university in designing the optical filters. The response to the mounting failures, from both the university and the company, was always the same: 'What you want to do is impossible.' This was interesting to me, as the French have a common expression, 'Impossible n'est pas *français,*' which means, 'There is no such thing as *can't* in French.' In other words, 'Nothing is impossible.'

Following two months of failed customer tests and a series of fruitless discussions, the company's executives and engineering design team proposed greatly decrementing the performance specifications of the device and drastically reducing the selling price, which would result in an essentially useless product that no company would buy. After all, who wants to obtain a savings of forty percent on the purchase price of a device that is unusable?

At this point, I decided to try a completely different approach. I had already deduced that the optical color filters were the source of the problem. Beginning with a local camera store catering to professional photographers, I investigated various materials that could be used as replacement filters. My next stop was a video camera shop, which then led me to a theatrical supply company where I discovered the colored cellophane 'gels' used to filter spotlights in dramatic productions. Purchasing a range of gels for each of the filter colors, I went back to the office to experiment until the optimal combination was found.

Taking pieces of cellophane and cutting them with scissors to fit the filter trays, my team tested the unit across a wide variety of gas charts demonstrating to our satisfaction that the cheap and simple fix worked. We then proceeded to cut gel filters for all the units in service with additional samples for the company's R&D facility in Europe, to be sent the next day by FedEx. The total materials cost for retrofitting all units was under twenty-five dollars, and the gel media satisfactorily corrected the problems, ultimately serving as a permanent replacement for the original custom manufactured optical glass filters. This innovation also saved nearly a thousand dollars per unit in manufacturing costs.

Degrading the performance specification was not the answer. Changing the mindset of 'impossible' into 'possible' was. The entire problem could have been avoided if the company's leadership had, from the beginning, maintained unrelenting design authority over the project. During development, rather than requiring the R&D team to meet the known U.S. performance parameters, they were permitted to unrealistically limit the range of variation in gas well charts used for establishing the design specification and testing when, in actual fact, real world gas charts were anything but consistent.

Innovation efforts, whether for products, services, processes, systems or methods should be subject to frequent, no-holds barred design reviews to assure accountability of the innovation team. A vast difference exists between 'freedom' in how an innovation goal is met and 'license' to relax standards in an attempt to compensate for a lack of creativity, ingenuity and sheer willpower in overcoming barriers.

Other important considerations in fostering an environment conducive for Giraffe innovators include:

1. Openness

In consulting with numerous organizations domestically and internationally over many years, I have encountered a broad disparity in terms of openness to new ideas. In forward thinking companies, the leadership labors to establish a receptive atmosphere where ideas can be freely discussed without defensiveness in regard to the ownership of those ideas. In these organizations, ideas are welcomed from any source, inside, outside, top, middle or bottom — the origin of the idea makes no difference, only its value.

Great ideas can come from the most unlikely sources. An example comes to mind from early in my career. Years ago, I attended a church where I met a man who was the Vice President of Engineering for a large food processing company with plants around the country. He was a very quiet person who rarely spoke about himself.

In time, I learned that he and his wife had grown up on farms in the Midwest, completed high school, married young, started a family, and embarked upon their own farming venture. Over the course of those years, they adopted several Native American children, adding to the number of mouths to feed. They also had the misfortune to experience a severe drought and consequently lost the farm. They were, however, fortunate enough to purchase another smaller farm and begin anew, but were then wiped out by a second drought. The third time has to be a charm, they certainly must have thought. But not for them. This time they lost everything. Well into their 40s and in dire financial straits, they moved to the city, looking for a way to support their large family. He was seeking employment with a resume that read:

Education: High school diploma

Work Experience:

1. Farmer - Drought, crops lost, farm failed.

2. Farmer - Drought, crops lost, farm failed.

3. Farmer - Drought, crops lost, farm failed, BROKE!

It certainly was no easy task for him to find a job. Eventually he did, in the maintenance department of a food processing plant. One day while tending to his duties, he observed a large contingent of 'suits' coming his way. When they were very near, they stopped. It was the CEO, Vice President of Engineering, several plant engineers and a group of consulting engineers. As he continued working, he could hear their discussion, which related to emission controls that would soon need to be installed.

After a while the discussion died down and the group prepared to move on. Approaching the group, he politely said, 'I couldn't help overhearing your discussion. I wanted to tell you that the solution you were discussing will not work in this particular application.' The group was stunned. After the initial shock, the VP of Engineering approached him and curtly asked, 'And who are you?' He responded with his name and the fact that he worked in the plant maintenance department. The VP responded, 'And what is your education?' He answered, 'high school.' By now the VP was both embarrassed and annoyed. Just as he was about to conclude the conversation with some sharp words for him to mind his own business, the CEO intervened. Stepping forward he cut in, saying to the group: 'You move along and I will join you presently.' His directive broke the tension, and the group moved on with the VP muttering something disparaging to an associate, certain that the maintenance man was about to be reprimanded by the CEO.

However, he was quite mistaken. Instead, the CEO pulled over a crate, sat down and said, 'Tell me why you think it won't work.' The farmer explained as the CEO listened intently. When he was done, the CEO asked him, 'If you never went to college, how did you learn these things?' He related that he had been a very financially challenged farmer who could not afford to buy much of the equipment and machinery needed, so he had learned to make-do. The CEO then asked him, what it would cost to build a small proof of principle pilot project of his idea for the emissions control system. The investment was around $25,000 which, in the late 1960s, was still real money. The CEO authorized the expenditure, over the very vocal and angry protests of the VP of engineering. When the prototype was completed and tested, it worked just as the maintenance man had said it would. The next step was to scale up to full plant size and from there to a system for installation in each of the corporation's numerous processing plants.

And that is how the failed farmer eventually became the new VP of Engineering for a very large food processing corporation. Although the farmer had no formal training, he possessed natural engineering ability as well as a brilliantly inquisitive mind, something that no degree can provide. With his innovative mindset teamed with the company's professional engineers, the 'farmer turned VP' could accomplish anything the corporation needed.

We can easily fall into the trap of believing that valuable ideas and innovations can come only from the 'designated keepers' of a specific field of knowledge. Not so. Does a framed certificate hanging on the wall guarantee intellectual aptitude? Knowledge perhaps, but not a questioning mind. During the Industrial Revolution (circa 1750-1850), a key factor in British manufacturing's leap ahead progress can be owed to an intriguing dynamic. At that time, scientific inquiry cut across all classes, allowing skilled craftsmen to collaborate with scholars and generate exponential outcomes.

When we are seeking breakthrough innovations, we should certainly look to those with specific expertise in that particular field. However, it is a colossal mistake to assume that no one else, either inside or outside of your organization or industry, might be capable of a truly ingenious solution. Do you recall the open source appeal of the National Inventors' Council which produced numerous innovative solutions implemented during World War II? (See the Preface.)

I have only made cursory mention of the term *open innovation*, as that is a subject I will cover in depth in a later book of this series on the process of innovation. However, for those who are unfamiliar with the concept of open innovation, it simply means looking outside for the inspiration and genesis of potentially innovative ideas. But outside of where? Outside of your organization and your industry.

Some organizations are closed to the concept of open innovation, wrongly believing that their business or industry is so specialized that no one outside of it could possibly contribute a valid idea for advancement. In decades of international consulting, I have worked with an extremely wide range of organizations including nonprofit, government and all types of businesses. The industries I have served are diverse, ranging from aerospace and defense to medical, professional services, machine shops and fabricators, research and development to food and pharmaceuticals. I cannot remember one that did not think that what their organization did was unique, at least to their industry. And they were right. Each was definitely quite unique. However, the problems they struggled with and the opportunities that awaited them were in many ways very similar.

More than 2,800 years ago, wise King Solomon declared, 'There is nothing new under the sun.' Since that time, industry and technology have greatly progressed, but fundamentally these words still ring true. The notion that we must continually 'reinvent the wheel' to meet the needs and objectives of our specific organization or industry is absurd, especially in a day when access to information is ubiquitous. We can and should avail ourselves of opportunities to learn from others. The world is filled with bright, ingenious people. No organization, industry or country has a corner on talent.

In the 1970's, benchmarking came into vogue — the practice of comparing your own organization against the best in your industry. From such exercises, many organizations gained valuable insights for improvements that could be easily adapted. Although useful, such activities were only capable of achieving incremental gains.

Every organization, is like a small pond, containing a limited amount of information, knowledge and experience. Each industry is like a lake, made of up of many small ponds containing substantially broader information, knowledge and experience, but the world is a vast ocean, containing an inexhaustible supply of information, knowledge and experience. Open innovation is the practice of seeking out the best information, knowledge and experience available, regardless of origin.

Within your organization alone there exists a wealth of untapped information, knowledge and experience. Much of it may not seem directly applicable to your business, but a surprising amount could be useful in fueling the innovation process. In the example of my European client, it was an avocational interest in photography that sent me to the camera store hunting replacement materials for the optical filters, as I was already familiar with the optical filters used on camera lenses and in darkrooms. In the end, optical filters were not the solution. Gel sheets from the theatrical supply store saved the day, but had I not known enough about photography to give me a starting point, it is unlikely I would have found the solution in the course of a single afternoon. What treasures of non-job related information, knowledge and experience do your people possess that might be the impetus for devising the innovations your organization needs?

Open innovation encompasses every potential information source for ideation, from the hobbies and interests of your people to the invention or creative idea gleaned from an unrelated industry halfway around the world. Giraffes understand that the outside world is teeming with concepts, methodologies, systems and inventions that could infuse new thinking into your organization. For Giraffes, the world is a vast playground for creating, finding, and combining powerful new ideas which can be transformed and developed into breakthrough innovations.

2. Culture

Obviously *openness* depends upon the organization's culture. However, the productivity of Giraffes can also be impacted by other aspects of an organization's culture.

Process — Is the atmosphere one of freedom or rather is 'control' a key factor in executive leadership and management style? Does the process of how the work is done really matter, as long as it does indeed get done with the best possible results? Some organizations run things 'by-the-book,' whereas others are more *laissez faire*. Unfortunately, while organizations reliant on prescribed action may have seamless operations, where every action is prescribed, the innovation process is certain to be stifled.

The fact is that when the all important question *'Why?'* ceases to be asked, innovation cannot progress. Organizations of all types and functions are best served where those who regularly solve problems are allowed to experiment with better methods. It is not a matter of throwing out the *rules* and operating by the 'seat of your pants,' but rather knowing when to 'bend' or 'circumvent' the *rules* to produce innovation.

Of course there is merit in systemizing very routine operations through the franchise model approach, where all variation is removed from a process in order to make it highly repeatable, with identical results. For example, a machine shop producing huge numbers of identical parts from CNC machines or a local fast food franchise where the jobs are staffed by low skilled workers and employee turnover is rampant would fit this model. However, it is an inappropriate model where job descriptions entail any kind of individual thinking or resourcefulness.

Interrelationships — If we fail to perceive the overall company as an organism of mutually dependent, interrelated systems, we will fall short of the target in designing new operational systems. Early in my career, I worked for a company whose chairman was much enamored with the then 'Big Eight' accounting and consulting firms. Eventually, he retained one of them to reorganize the product accounting and billing functions. A six-figure project was sold to the chairman by a pair of sleek, gray-haired foxes, senior partners in the firm. However, their team of twenty-five year old, newly minted MBA consultants who did the actual assignment, had little previous real life work experience prior to joining the consulting firm. To their credit, they performed what they believed to be an exhaustive study of every function in the designated departments before deciding to change *everything* and implement an entirely new system for improved efficiency. Chaos ensued and, within a year, all of the product accounting and billing functions were back to being performed in the original way.

Why? Because, although the young consultants had documented and studied the existing system, they had not fully understood the intricate relationships between the various steps and functions. When it came to operations, the new system was not nearly as efficient as the old one, which had been systematically developed over time by employees who were actually performing the work. With all of their detailed analysis, the *rookies* had missed the proverbial 'forest for the trees.' This failure may have resulted from the fact that observing and interviewing someone who does a task is simply not the same as doing the task yourself.

I am not a golfer, ever only played twice, but if I spent a few days following a pro-golfer and scrutinizing his every move, it would be pretty naive of me to expect that when I stepped up to swing a club I would be much more likely to hit the ball straight than I am today. The young consultants thought they understood what was being done, yet they obviously did not spend enough time interviewing employees and observing their daily functions to fully comprehend the reasoning and rationale behind their home-grown methodology.

Teamwork — A culture can also be corrupted when there are factions, competing or even warring for turf control and recognition. For real innovation to thrive, everyone has to be on *one team* with common objectives and goals, staying focused on the common good of the organization and everyone in it. Like an arrow to the heart, divisiveness kills innovation. Innovation flourishes where cooperation rather than competitiveness abounds.

One company promoting a culture of cooperation is Pinstripe, Inc., a Recruitment Process Outsourcing (RPO) professional services firm, led by an executive team of five women, has swiftly climbed to the top of its field. In the economic fallout from the recession of 2008, many large corporations so downsized their Human Resources departments that they were no longer able to cope with the hiring needs of their organizations. At that time, Pinstripe sensed an opportunity, took the risk and chose to expand. As an RPO company, they offered a win-win solution. Partnering with Pinstripe, corporations could acquire a dedicated talent acquisition team serving as an extension of their hard-pressed HR departments. This allows their clients to streamline processes and improve business results while raising the caliber of new hires — all without increasing the fixed costs of their HR budgets.

Pinstripe has doubled its revenue every twelve to eighteen months since its founding in 2005, growing at the rate of more than fifty percent annually, nearly double the industry average. The company now has 450 employees and expects to continue the growth trend. CEO, Sue Marks attributes the organization's on-going success to strategic investments in talent, technology, and infrastructure.

What are the keys to this explosive growth? Inspiring a passion for excellence in the services provided to clients is critical. It is their view that Pinstripe actually has two clients: the company retaining their services and the candidates they recruit. Pinstripe represents the client company to the individuals being recruited, with all contacts, emails, phone calls and even interviews being conducted in the client's name, thus serving as a true extension of the client organization's HR team

The Pinstripe Impression Center, responsible for fielding all applicant emails and call backs, focuses on the candidate *experience*, ensuring that each applicant has an available resource for questions or updates during the hiring process. Modeled after the service delivery expertise refined by Zappos, Pinstripe's Talent Relationship Management technology platform serves to create a thoroughly positive candidate experience. In a day when many HR functions use software to prescreen applicants, with rejected applicants rarely receiving any notification, much less feedback, supporting and valuing potential candidates leaves a highly favorable impression. It also allows Pinstripe to build a database of prospective applicants for the future.

Corporate culture is a top priority for the Pinstripe executive team. In an effort to retain the 'small company feel,' they have pursued various technologies as the organization has grown. Maintaining communication that includes everyone is of vital importance. Posters can be seen throughout Pinstripe's corporate headquarters espousing Pinstripe's vision of *Boldly Changing the Way the World Views Talent* and core values:

Be Passionate & Dynamic

Build Trust & Credibility

Drive to Get Results

Foster Collaboration

Embrace Innovation & Resourcefulness

They are passionate about these values. In fact, each meeting begins with an opportunity for individuals to recognize their colleagues for actions which demonstrate those values.

Pinstripe's hiring criteria has been central to the company's success. They hire people who are highly motivated and have a knack for finding creative solutions. Marks believes that, 'Our success is a testament to the caliber and dedication of our employees. Every day our people take on the most complex talent acquisition challenges and deliver solutions, ensuring that clients get the talent they need.'

To attract and retain top talent, the executive team has made training and development key to every employee's experience at Pinstripe. The organization strives to provide opportunities for growth and career advancement. To foster collaboration between client teams and across specialty areas, Pinstripe has developed 'Centers of Expertise,' where recruitment specialists can share ideas and practices as well as consulting with colleagues on the challenges they face, to further enhance recruiting excellence.

Marks believes that their organization must continually move forward, taking calculated risks as part of the process. They may not always get it right the first time, as Marks says, 'We make mistakes, but we keep learning from them.' Employing innovative approaches for better performance is Pinstripe's modus operandi. Nor is the organization reluctant to embrace the concept of Creative Destruction. Angela Hills, Executive Vice President states, 'We are not afraid to rip it apart and start fresh,' creatively destroying old paradigms that no longer fit their marketplace. They recognize that traditional methods of talent acquisition must be broken so something fresh can emerge.

The Pinstripe leadership team is not afraid of the challenge. They are continually driving change through aggressive innovation, adding value to client relationships through innovative thinking and practices. Is it any wonder that they have so quickly risen to become market leaders in their industry?

Then how important really is culture? That's an interesting question that has almost as many answers as there are organizations. The problem is that while most senior executives are able to state an opinion, in the vast majority of cases, their opinion does not correlate with the reality of their organization. But there are those where the two are closely aligned.

Take Zappos, which Pinstripe seeks to emulate. Here is what Tony Hsieh, Zappos CEO has to say about commitment to culture in reality, not just words.

What's the best way to build a brand for the long term?

In a word: culture.

At Zappos, our belief is that if you get the culture right, most of the other stuff — like great customer service, or building a great long-term brand, or passionate employees and customers — will happen naturally on its own.

We believe that your company's culture and your company's brand are really just two sides of the same coin. The brand may lag the culture at first, but eventually it will catch up.

Your culture is your brand.

If Hsieh is right, what does that say about your brand?

3. Esprit de Corps

This is the French term for 'shared spirit.' When I visit an organization's office, it takes me only a few minutes to sense whether or not there is a positive spirit and camaraderie. Some companies simply exude team spirit. Think Southwest Airlines or a direct sales company like Shaklee. Employees of these companies are so 'fired-up' and proud to be a part of the organization, that they cannot wait to show it. How do I know the spirit when I enter a company's office for the first time? People smile. They are happy to be there. I hear laughter and upbeat conversation — people clearly enjoying themselves at work. I have never been able to understand why this should not be the case everywhere. Spirit costs nothing! Or, from another perspective, *the lack of it could cost everything.*

Espirit de corps requires no real monetary investment, besides the small cost of supporting coffee and donuts, cook-out days, and other morale building events. What it does require is a commitment to valuing people. Far too often, leaders seem to forget that, 'You can fool some of the people all of the time and all of the people some of the time, but you can't fool *all* of the people *all* of the time.' The point is that it does not take long for employees to figure out whether the organization's leaders truly value them as people or are merely paying them lip service in order to keep them working as hard as possible for as little as possible for as long as possible. Genuine team spirit creates a positive dynamic which promotes both creativity and lasting productivity.

Recently, I spent nearly a week with American Electric Power Company's River Operations Group. Whether sitting in the board room with the executive team or talking with boat captains and deck hands on the tow boats, I discovered that here were some of the happiest, yet hardest working employees I had ever met. They literally love the company. Extremely loyal, they are among the most productive employees in their industry. Consistent with their culture, the River Operations Group makes safety a first priority. They are the first to shut down river operations when fog or other dangerous river conditions warrant. This unwavering commitment to safety is impressive because, with over ninety boats and thirty-two-hundred barges, shutting down river operations for even an hour is very costly.

With a leadership motto of: *Leading Forward — Maximizing Results — Fostering Teamwork & Bringing Out the Best* and a corporate culture characterized by the statement: *High Involvement — Collaboration — Mutual Care — Shared Commitment & Agility,* AEP River Operations is an organization that understands and values the competitive power of applied innovation.

As the clear innovation leader within their industry, AEP River Operations was awarded the prestigious '2011 Work Boat Environmental Initiative Award.' The 2011 redesign and retrofit of their first *green* boat the *M/V Donna Rushing*, resulted in over one hundred unique innovations. The *Donna Rushing* is now the poster child for *greening* the inland waterways industry. Far from being a small, family owned, 'folksy' enterprise, AEP River Operations has over fourteen-hundred-fifty employees and operations spanning six fleet operations scattered across the eastern and central part of the nation. In 2010, the company moved over seventy million tons of cargo for its customers. Owned by American Electric Power, a publicly traded corporation and the largest electric utility in the United States, it convincingly demonstrates that large, publicly owned companies need not be faceless, uncaring, bureaucratic monoliths. AEP River Operations is precisely the opposite. Without a single exception, every person I met at AEP River Operations expressed a high level of pride, in both the work they do and in being a part of the organization.

While the loyalty and spirit of these employees is commendable, it begs the question, why this optimism and exuberance cannot be commonplace? Sadly, organizations like AEP River Operations represent a rare exception among today's large corporations. Giraffes flourish in organizations that choose to develop their people, invest in them and create an atmosphere where they can enjoy their work and thrive.

4. Rewards

This seems to be the one of the most daunting issues facing business leaders. In general, rewards ultimately come down to compensation, and therein lies the problem. What happens when innovations become blockbusters that fill the coffers of the corporation? Are those directly responsible for these results permitted to share in the benefits, regardless of where they may fit into the organizational hierarchy?

A technology company based in the U.K. for whom I provided consulting services on defense and aerospace programs for many years, decided at one point to implement a suggestion box to gather ideas for possible innovations. The employees were promised that any innovations which were implemented would result in a percentage payout over the life of the innovation to whoever had made the suggestion. The possibility of financial rewards both excited and motivated the employees. Almost immediately, suggestions began pouring in. Within the first week, it became clear that one of the employee proposed innovations was an obvious blockbuster. What happened next? The following Monday, the suggestion box disappeared. A memo was circulated stating that the suggestions received had been of insufficient merit to justify continuing the program. Six months passed and the very same innovation which had been suggested was suddenly implemented. It was announced as an idea of the senior management and therefore, the issue of payout was never raised. Can you imagine the impact these actions had on company morale, not to mention the lack of future employee proffered innovations? Yes, the company may have saved the money it would have paid out in a reward formula (in this instance, a considerable sum) but what did it lose in terms of additional, potentially successful innovations in the following weeks, months, and years – not to mention a sharp decline in morale and the likely loss of disaffected talent? Was it really worth it?

Giraffe innovators flourish in an environment where leadership encourages, and even demands, exceptional creativity and personal commitment. In response, however, company leadership *must* recognize and reward individual achievement. The freedom to explore outside-the-box alternatives ignites the imagination. Giraffes possess a contagious enthusiasm. Teams learn to reach high — very high in the company of Giraffes. In his book, *The Steve Jobs Way*, Jay Elliot, former Senior Vice President of Apple, writes that Steve Jobs' commitment to achieving excellence was an inspiration to everyone around him. Elliot maintains that Apple's success was largely due to Jobs' vision of making products simple and easy to operate, a task which was by no means 'simple' to accomplish. As Apple's co-founder, Steve Wozniak could certainly affirm, this 'happens through creativity and innovations with a relentless pursuit of perfection. It means thinking through everything with the laser-focused goal of making it [the product] intuitive to the user.' Jobs insisted that if you need a manual, you haven't designed it right and, 'the more he [Steve Jobs] advanced, the simpler his products became.' Steve Jobs believed that, 'Great products come from people who are passionate. Great products only come from teams that are passionate.' For Jobs, they were not just products, but extensions of who he was. He set high standards for himself and everyone around him because, as he put it, 'You only get to do a limited number of things in your life.'

Giraffes prosper in organizations where they can make those things count!

Giraffe Example:

Norma McCulloch

Necessity is the Mother of Invention. (Her Favorite Saying)

One of New Zealand's best known innovators, Norma McCulloch was an 'ideas' person; she was always devising something new. In 2003, she was named one of the 'World's Top 10 Women Inventors for the Best Community Invention' by the Global Women Inventors and Innovators Network. This honor was conferred on her for her creation of the 'Breath of Life Resuscitator' used in CPR.

Norma was a lifelong innovator and inventor. Born in Liverpool, England in 1933, she went to work in a factory at the age of fifteen to help support her family. She began inventing in her childhood and continued to solve a wide variety of problems throughout life. At the age of thirty, she emigrated with her husband and family to New Zealand in search of a better climate to aid her recovery from tuberculosis.

McCulloch became a television celebrity in the 1960s as an expert on the then 'new art' of freezing food. Her *Deep Freeze Cookery* book sold 200,000 copies. One of her early innovations, a hand pump for extracting air from freezer bags, was later modified to 'burp' water beds. Originally made from two simple, valved cardboard tubes, a subsequent dishwasher-safe model was developed in plastic. The pump sold throughout New Zealand, Australia, Great Britain, Canada, and the United States. A New Zealand press representative in London described McCulloch as 'a one-woman trade mission.' In addition to being an inventor, she was an astute marketer and promoter. As a result of her many product inventions, she created McCulloch Products Ltd., which began producing innovative cooking gadgets.

After retiring in 1993, from the company she had founded, McCulloch continued inventing innovative products. She invented, developed, and patented a new type of Linear Displacement Manual Resuscitator. The device was made of two telescoping plastic cylinders with a bi-directional valve, able to repeatedly deliver a measured amount of air, or air/oxygen blend, into a person's lungs in compliance with International Standard Requirements and American Heart Association Guidelines. Unlike traditional Bag Valve Masks (developed in the 1950s), it was easy-to-use, arrived fully assembled, and remained very affordable. This product was marketed in New Zealand, Australia, and the UK under the McCulloch Medical brand.

Later, in response to the need for a unit to resuscitate prematurely born calves, she created an easy-to-use Calf Resuscitator using the same technology as the unit designed for humans. This product proved so successful that an entire range of resuscitators were created for foals, lambs, piglets, llamas and alpacas, dogs, cats, and birds, as well as zoo animals. These inventions are also marketed through McCulloch Medical in thirty-two countries world-wide.

The Patented McCulloch Medical™ Animal Resuscitators have won numerous awards, including:

- Best Prototype - National Agricultural Field Days, New Zealand

- Best New Equipment - National Agricultural Field Days, New Zealand

- Best New Product - Royal Welsh Agricultural Show, UK

- D.L.G. Innovation Award - Eurotier, Germany

- Best New Product - Balmoral Royal Agricultural Show, Ireland

- Best Product of Show - Balmoral Royal Agricultural Show, Ireland

- Best Technical Innovation Award - Royal Highland Show, Edinburgh, Scotland

- First Prize Most Innovative Horse Care Product - Equitana, Louisville, Kentucky, USA

- Gold Medal International Exhibition of Inventions, Geneva, Switzerland

- SONY NZ Excellence in Innovation Award, New Zealand

Another clever product was a sheep wool duster, known as the 'chandelier duster,' which she marketed and sold in the United States, Canada, and Taiwan. Given New Zealand's large sheep production, this product proved a great boon to their national industry.

McCulloch absolutely insisted on high quality design standards which resulted in all of her products having a long life and people seldom needing to replace them. Indeed, customers have used her early freezer-bag pumps for as long as forty years without needing a replacement, and her resuscitator comes with a two year warranty.

As an inventor, she never became personally wealthy. Instead of profiting personally from her innovative inventions, she instead chose to invest back into her company. Over the years, she never stopped inventing useful and innovative products. Later in life, she created a modular 'en suite' bath, capable of being fitted into the existing plumbing of a house for bathing, thereby enabling elderly or disabled people to remain in their own homes rather than having to be relocated to other facilities.

Norma McCulloch's amazingly productive life is a testimony to the fact that lacking an advanced formal education is no bar to becoming a world-renowned innovator.

Chapter 5 — Thought Questions

1. Why are Giraffes hard to keep? What do they require to be productive?

2. Do we see protecting our Giraffes as critical to keeping them? What, if anything, does our organization do to protect them?

3. Do we see any 'spillover' from meeting Giraffes' needs to benefits accruing to other employees within our organization?

4. What organizational changes will be required to make our company an innovation friendly place conducive to achieving the results we need to create a sustainable future?

5. What would it cost our organization to create a Giraffe friendly environment? What will be the long term consequences of not doing so?

6. Has our organization experienced innovation initiatives that ended in the development of wonderfully creative ideas and possibly even products, services or internal changes, that brought no ROI value or payback? If so, why did this occur?

7. Does our organization have a track record of sacrificing 'what can be' for the expediency of 'getting it done'?

8. Does our organization make a clear distinction between active oversight and control of innovation initiatives to ensure the freedom of the innovation teams to explore and achieve the goals without burdensome restrictions or relaxing standards?

9. Is our organization 'open' to new ideas, even if they are unconventional or originate from a seemingly unlikely source?

10. From what sources is our organization presently drawing its ideas for innovation? Are many of these sources external to the team(s) tasked with creating the innovations? Are many of these sources external to our organization?

11. How would we describe our culture? If surveyed, how would our employees describe the culture particularly in regard to fostering open innovation?

12. Are our innovation teams operating with everyone on-board, playing one game, on one team, with one purpose and shared goal?

13. Do the Giraffe innovators and their teams within our organization receive the recognition and rewards that they deserve and which will continue to motivate them toward ever greater innovation achievements?

14. What attributes set Norma McCulloch's life apart as a foresighted and prolific innovator.

Never underestimate a Giraffe running at full gallop
with an extraordinary idea.

PART II   Giraffes to the Rescue

The question is not if opposition to innovation can be overcome, but whether there is the will and commitment to do so.

Chapter Six: Guarding Against the Enemies of Giraffes

In the wild, the giraffe's enemies are primarily lions and crocodiles. When danger threatens at the watering hole, giraffes are careful to protect one another. While a giraffe can crush a lion's skull with a single kick, not much else bothers these peaceful creatures.   In nature, giraffes don't really have a distinctive cry like other animals. Females frantically seeking lost calves can bellow, and courting males cough and make strange, flutelike sounds.   Giraffes travel in very loose, open herds and have no territorial inclinations.   Their tall and majestic stature makes them easy to spot.

Organizational Giraffes also have a way of 'standing out' in a crowd too! Creative personalities are often quirky – and Giraffes are no exception.   It can be frustrating to carry on a conversation with someone whose head is always 'in the clouds.' When they are *thinking*, Giraffes tend to be distracted, not always listening to what you have to say.   For the most part, however, they are very likable, often winning the respect of others through their high ideals, generosity, and optimism.

It's not that Giraffes try to make enemies within the organization.   It is a natural consequence of their mission and comes with the territory. Those enemies they do make can be formidable and, depending upon the organizational culture, even fierce.

Their enemies come in two forms. 'Predatory' people who in someway feel threatened and 'the system' or organization itself.   I'll begin with the predatory sort, as they are the most difficult for leadership to restrain.

Once an initiative is launched, Giraffes tend to be obstinate, strong-willed and relentless. Their single-minded determination to realize that innovation will likely offend and exasperate others. They are sometimes accused of being *prima donnas*. Where necessary, Giraffes can be brutally frank and quite tactless in maneuvering the political landscape. Giraffes who are consumed with 'getting it right' have also been known to push themselves and others beyond all reasonable limits. This is neither egotism nor ruthless ambition, but rather the evidence of a passion for perfection. True Giraffes are more outcome than recognition oriented. As their main objective is to create new dimensions of performance, they are highly driven and intent on attaining that goal. A Giraffe's greatest reward is in seeing the tangible results produced by their innovations.

This is not to infer that Giraffes will not be become upset if they never receive praise, recognition or financial rewards for their accomplishments. Whether or not they are 'people smart,' anyone capable of producing breakthrough innovation is also clever enough to know when they are being fleeced. Acutely aware of the benefits the organization reaps through them, Giraffes will expect appropriate recognition and compensation.

Enemies perceive Giraffes as favorites, granted special privileges and dispensation to break all the rules whenever they please. Sometimes, in order to put a company back on its feet or propel it forward, Giraffes must become agents of (temporary) disruption. When timing is crucial, they will frequently dispense with protocol and may show indifference to glaring social infractions. If necessary, Giraffes will disregard both warning signals and territorial boundaries. They may also incense others by arbitrarily 'borrowing' first-rate talent from wherever they can find it within the organization.

What peeved colleagues do not realize is that breakthrough opportunities can appear suddenly, demanding swift and immediate action, even split-second timing. They need to be appraised of how Giraffes think and operate and why they do what they do or else trouble ensues. Co-workers may also be envious of the attention and privileges accorded Giraffes. Adversaries may seek revenge through some form of sabotage or delaying tactics. Such 'interfering' with innovation could result in devastating consequences for the entire organization and its future. For Giraffes to successfully innovate on an ongoing basis, a CIO (Chief Innovation Officer) – or other well placed and deeply invested individual – must stand guard.

Some of the Giraffe's opponents honestly do not see the need for innovation. It is very hard for me to even conceive how it can be that, within organizations today, especially larger, more sophisticated corporations, there are people currently in leadership and management positions who still believe that they can prosper over the long term with a 'business as usual' approach.

Blind to the need for innovation, they may resent the Giraffe's continual pushing for change with the aim of realizing ever greater breakthrough innovations, utterly convinced that 'business as usual' is the right approach.

Hypothetically, opponents of innovation will acknowledge that change is necessary and that organizations cannot remain static in a fast-shifting marketplace. But their concept of change remains very slow, evolutionary and incremental. They are intransigent – determined to preserve the *status quo*, clinging to what is 'safe.' 'Don't change what works,' is their mantra. 'What the organization has done until now has worked or we would not be where we are today.' Such attitudes are dangerously short-sighted. Try telling that to the employees of Kodak, Borders Books or Harry & David! Businesses must learn to navigate a turbulent and uncertain future through strategic innovation and the requisite internal change.

Leaping into innovation's great unknown may seem precarious, but in a global world, fear, denial and inaction will destine your organization to falling further and further behind competitors. They will, eventually, 'eat your lunch.' In today's business climate, continuous innovation is the essential strategy for ensuring future sustainability.

Sometimes even more menacing to a Giraffe's performance and well-being is the organization itself. Giraffes flourish in an energetic, innovation-friendly environment. However, as I have already mentioned, there are elements within the organization which will resist the strategic necessity of innovation until it's too late. When the overall organizational climate gets icy, Giraffes can be frozen in their tracks!

Inertia paralyzes innovation. The larger the company, the greater the inertia. A well established, major corporation is like a large ocean liner. When an iceberg is sighted, the command to alter course may come quickly from the captain on the bridge. The engine room will also respond immediately, but an object in the ship's path can be riveting for alarmed passengers watching the drama unfold. Ever so slowly, almost imperceptibly – the huge vessel turns as the iceberg and impending collision loom ever nearer. Large organizations, whatever the industry, are like great, hulking ships and the larger the organization, the more slowly the ship is likely to change course without radical intervention.

Bureaucracy is the real enemy here, not the individuals involved. The sheer size and complexity of the departments and functions that must be mobilized and coordinated to affect change can be daunting. It makes little difference whether the structure is traditional, matrix or a blend. However, as I said before, it is imperative to the innovation effort that everyone be on-board, playing one game, on one team, with one purpose and shared goal. Where this is the culture, people are far less likely to be offended or throw sand in the gears and far more willing to get on-board when *rules* must be broken in order to seize an opportunity.

For example, most organizations periodically experience the need to make a payment to a vendor or customer who is unable to wait for the normal payment timeframe. In this case, someone at the top or near the top of the organizational ladder decides it will be done. And although checks are run only once a week, the decision is made that it must happen today, this afternoon…

now! What follows? Someone prepares the check request form, right away. It is walked through the building to an executive who signs off. Then it is hand-carried to the person appointed to print checks. And, yes, even though the system must physically print a minimum of twenty-five paper checks at a time, it is done, with all but the one check then voided. 'What a terrible waste of paper checks!' some may cry. But does it really matter how many checks were voided? What matters is that someone in leadership understood what had to be done, made the necessary call and the one, the single, crucial check needed was issued.

This is precisely the attitude we must have for innovation to thrive. Unfortunately, all too often we become focused on the twenty-four checks that had to be sacrificed to realize the one. If the one was truly important, then the wasted checks are an infinitesimal price to pay. We must always maintain our perspective. What is the big picture? What is our goal? Is it smoothness of operations? Preserving the *status quo* and keeping risk to a minimum will not produce the innovations necessary to make your organization a marketplace leader.

Too many of our organizations have grown and bureaucratized to become like the Borg of Star Trek fame, a mindless and interconnected collective assimilating into itself any and all intelligence it encounters. The Borg existed for the sole purpose of perpetuating the Borg. Within many organizations, a Borg mentality pervades. However, assimilating everything and everyone into one complacent, homogenous mass is not conducive to Giraffe innovators nor to achieving the breakthrough innovations which will create sustainability.

Effective leadership has the power to declaw and neutralize a Giraffe's enemies. The question is not *if* opposition to innovation can be overcome, but whether there is the *will* and *commitment* to do so. As I stated earlier, although many executive leaders have loudly sung the praises of innovation, few have taken the necessary steps to activate this powerful catalyst for creating sustainable growth.

Why the disconnect in the executive suite? I believe the cause is twofold. First, there exists a pervasive lack of real understanding as to what innovation truly is, how it is accomplished and the magnitude of the benefits that can accrue to the organization through recurring waves of breakthrough innovation. For too many, innovation is still a fuzzy concept with all of the hype only adding to the confusion.

The second source of reluctance lies in the issue of 'commitment.' Sadly, we live in a day when results are judged by quarterly performance, if not monthly. Stocks rise and fall precipitously at the slightest hint of news, good or bad. Despite all the talk in the business press about 'sustainability,' none of this takes us any closer toward realizing this goal.

To build something vibrant, lasting and sustainable, the strategic perspective from the executive suite cannot be short term. Can you imagine a contractor building a house that way, when all that mattered were each day's results? If, like today's investors, the contractor and every subcontractor concerned themselves solely with immediate results, such as collecting daily progress payments on work completed, what would happen?   Each subcontractor would rush to finish as much work as possible each day. Good, you might think…initially. The house will be finished faster. But not so.

Just imagine...the landscapers hurry to get there first, because they have a hole in their schedule and need cash flow. They finish grade the property and plant all of the foundation shrubbery where the house is staked out. Next, the foundation contractor arrives to dig the hole, destroying all of the finish grading and landscaping. The same day, he begins pouring concrete for the basement and foundation walls. But let's not forget the plumber, who arrives to find that he cannot install the drain tile and water and sewer laterals without boring holes through the freshly poured concrete. Bright and early the next morning, the carpenter crew arrives to begin constructing walls on top of the foundation, before the concrete has fully cured. Then the dry wallers show up to begin their work, enclosing and finishing the interior walls. But, when the plumber returns with the electrician and HVAC subcontractor, to their dismay, they find that they must tear holes in all of the newly completed walls in order to do their work. Lastly, it rains on the nearly completed house, before the roofing contractor arrives on the job site.

The upshot would be totally nonsensical, and the resulting house, if ever finished, would be vastly over budget and well past the scheduled completion date —a house you would never want to live in. Yet, helter-skelter is exactly how we are running many of our organizations, especially public companies. It is time that CEO's, boards of directors, stock analysts and shareholders say 'enough.' Maybe, it is time to take the innovative step of doing away with quarterly reporting, altogether, for public corporations. This may seem drastic, but unless a method of ending the current fixation with short term results is found, there will be no path left for moving our public corporations toward true sustainability.

Commitment is not a four-letter word. Rather than merely paying it lip service, the leaders of our organizations need to take the fight for innovation seriously. They need to rethink, regroup, and make the long term commitments necessary to transform their organizations into innovation-friendly environments, where Giraffes can consistently produce real innovation.

Giraffe Example:

Robert Jordan

Nothing is more motivating than having someone pay you for a device that you thought up, engineered and built.

Idle Free Systems is a perfect illustration of just how much can be achieved by a single person who is passionately committed to making the world a better place. Idle Free's founder and president, Robert Jordan, drove a long haul truck for twenty years. Over the course of this career, he spent over 6,000 nights sleeping in the cab bunk of his truck, listening to the persistent sound of its diesel engine idling. He frequently wondered if trucks could be redesigned to use less fuel and generate less pollution. It is estimated that idling trucks in North America alone waste upwards of one billion gallons of fuel annually.

Eventually, Jordan decided to experiment with this idea, using his own Mack truck as a laboratory. The result was a series of new and innovative, breakthrough technologies that allow the transfer of excess energy from the tractor and refrigerated trailer to sealed batteries stored inside the truck. Jordan's inventions culminated in the issue of a new patent in late 2006 and the creation of Idle Free Systems, a company utilizing these patented ideas to build fuel saving idle-elimination systems. This patented technology system allows drivers to use stored energy from the truck's engine and, where available, its reefer (trailer refrigeration) unit, to heat or cool the bunk or cab, warm the engine or fuel tanks to prevent the diesel fuel from gelling in very cold weather, and meet the driver's basic hotel needs – including television and microwave with 120 volt AC electricity.

In 2006, Jordan stopped driving trucks in order to devote all of his time to the company. Two years later, Jordan hired a CEO. This enabled Jordan to focus his energies on continuing system innovation as Chief Technology Officer of Idle Free Systems.

Today, the Idle Free electric Auxiliary Power Unit (APU) with Reefer Link technology is the only reefer-based idle elimination system on the market. The Idle Free electric APU is unique for many reasons, one of the most significant being that it runs on alternating current (AC).

In 2009, Idle Free Systems introduced a new patent-pending A/C unit for the Idle Free electric APU. The new system is more efficient than its predecessor, running 10 hours or more (instead of 8-10) on fewer batteries (4 instead of 5). In addition, the new A/C unit reduced overall system installation time to approximately eight hours — half the installation time required for other systems. Robert Jordan's innovations have significantly upgraded on-the-job living conditions for truck drivers as well as saving large quantities of fuel, reducing pollution and extending engine life by preventing 'wear and tear' from needless engine idling.

I believe that education as most see it stops or slows down innovation.

Certain professions are taught as if everything previous is correct.

This leaves a person confused about opportunities.

How many people leave/finish school and see a road in front of them?

The map they look for does not exist.

The key is trial and error, education by mistake, turn around when you encounter a dead end.

Learn from your mistakes, learn to move forward.

A pat on the back is really a push to continue.

If no one will pay for your idea, it is just an idea.

I do not want to be on my customers white boards.

I want to be taken for granted.

I want to be a solution to their problems, not another problem on their white board.

Passion comes from respect.

Respect comes from hard work.

Hard work is easy when you realize that you make a difference.

Making money is not as important as earning money.

You are judged by what you do, not by what you say.

– Robert Jordan

Chapter 6 — Thought Questions

1. What are the two major enemies of Giraffes?

2. In what ways are they also enemies of innovation?

3. Why are Giraffes frequently targeted as enemies by some people within their own organization?

4. Why do Giraffes require 'special privileges'? What are those 'special privileges' and how are they perceived by others within our organization?

5. Why do Giraffes view timing as being so crucial to successful innovation?

6. How important, is continuous, breakthrough innovation to the future of our organization?

7. What are the greatest institutional obstacles to company-wide, continuous innovation within our organization?

8. How does our organizational culture resemble the Borg? How does our organization differ?

9. Within our organization, is there a close connection between the leadership's 'commitment' to open innovation and the reality of its occurrence? Is the leadership of our organization committed to long term strategic and sustainable outcomes or fixated on short term results?

10. What is my equivalent to 6,000 nights spent in the cab bunk? What problem, issue, or opportunity is waiting for me to solve?

11. What characteristics of Robert Jordan's life most impress me as being hallmarks of a successful Giraffe innovator?

Leaders need to realize that Giraffes function best in an environment which boosts creative thinking, advances the free exchange of ideas and encourages collaboration.

Chapter Seven: Keeping Giraffes on the Reserve

In Africa's spacious grasslands, giraffes like nothing better than munching on the soft leaves of the acacia tree. They are magnificent trees, reaching heights of up to forty feet. Acacias have lacy, fern-like leaves and gorgeous yellow and white blossoms. Giraffes love their Acacias. They are non-territorial and social, living in loose, open herds (usually from two to fifteen), all moving in the same general direction. The herds are considered 'open' because no set rules exist to keep them from moving in and out of different herds. Most of a giraffe's hydration comes from the condensation which gathers on and is absorbed by leaves. While they prefer to do their nibbling on familiar ground, climate disruptions such as drought can force them to move elsewhere. They can also be driven away by a shortage of forage or an increase in natural predators.

Organizational Giraffes can be driven off by the winds of change. Always on the look-out for marketplace opportunities, Giraffes can easily be caught off guard by a shift in company policy. If leadership begins to hamper their efforts or, worse yet, cuts off the funding needed to create their magic, that is a sign of 'climate' disruption, or if Giraffes find themselves repeatedly ambushed by organizational predators, they will consider their options. Consequently, your Giraffes may decide to flee the reserve, en masse. Giraffes tend to be apolitical and generally averse to the backbiting and subterfuge of office warfare. Where office intrigues abound, most Giraffes will quickly beat a path to the door or at the very least choose to bide their time, adopting a low, non-innovating profile.

True Giraffes target the achievement of breakthrough innovations for increased profitability. As this can only be accomplished through the successful development of new and innovative products and services, or internal changes, Giraffes who are being blocked at every turn will not be happy. Top performers will quickly seek more favorable conditions. To prevent this, leadership must be hawk-eyed and ever mindful regarding the 'care and feeding' of Giraffes. As a steady flow of innovations is critical to the organization's future, leaders should value their Giraffes, providing encouragement, protection, resources and appropriate compensation. Smart leaders will be certain to generously compensate Giraffes for their achievements. In business, appreciation should always come with a dollar sign attached. Praise is appreciated, but financial remuneration says it best. That will keep the sun shining for your Giraffes.

As I have previously mentioned, wild giraffes have voracious appetites, typically feeding sixteen to twenty hours a day, and consuming up to one hundred-forty pounds of food daily. Similarly, resources are key to keeping Giraffe innovators from seeking greener pastures. Organizational Giraffes will slowly starve without the resources breakthrough innovations require to become reality. For continuing success, executives must cultivate an environment which feeds their creative powers.

The 'food' Giraffes crave comes in the form of mental stimuli and visual surroundings play a vital role. A sterile office environment can result in boredom and dishearten not only the highly creative within your organization, but everyone. Studies have confirmed that from early childhood on, our surroundings greatly influence our moods, mindset and level of creative output. I find it disturbing to drive past a modern school building with hardly any windows and an architecture so totally unimaginative that it looks more like a prison than a learning center. Is this the best we can do for the nurture and development of young minds?

Hopefully, your organization does not suffer from an office building with all the ambience of an IRS waiting room. Even if nothing can be done about the building's exterior, there is no reason to despair. With a little creative effort and a minimal investment, you can still work wonders to revamp the interior. Take small actions to begin with, then wait to see how people respond. After even minor changes, you will be amazed at the positive feedback. Redecorating for the purpose of stimulating creativity has the additional benefit of sending employees the message that you care about them and want their environment to be interesting and attractive.

Why bother? The client offices I visit range from elegant to dumpy, visually exciting to deadly dull. If you have ever seen the movie *Joe Versus the Volcano* starring Tom Hanks and Meg Ryan, the opening scene depicts Joe's (the main character) dreary place of employment. The movie is a satire and hysterically funny but sadly, in some respects, not that far from the truth.

To be fair, most offices today are nicely appointed; yet despite the attempt, the end result is dismally unexciting. On entering, it becomes immediately obvious that the designer followed a stock formula, starting with a base color whether mauve, tan or gray (the current 'in' colors) – followed by the selection of two or three accent colors, some generic wall hangings and color-coordinated furnishings. This, together with the practical, but acutely uninspiring fluorescent lighting, does little to stimulate the mind. It is all so run-of-the-mill; it puts you to sleep. An environment deprived of passion and imagination cannot inspire creativity.

Our mindsets can be greatly affected by color, design, patterns, textures as well as imaginative lighting – both an art and science in itself. Sound and smell can be employed to soothe or energize. Oddly, organizations who spend fortunes to generate 'outside-the-box' thinking often forget to consider the setting. Too often, having never given a thought to surroundings, executives are left scratching their heads as to what went wrong when the return on their innovation investment proves disappointing.

Leaders need to realize that Giraffes function best in an environment which boosts creative thinking, advances the free exchange of ideas and encourages collaboration. Steve Jobs built a spectacular atrium with a grand piano for his development teams. But then, he was a Giraffe. Whether or not you are a Giraffe, you must learn to understand how these individuals think in order to capture their creative energies.

A few years ago, a Fortune 50 company launched an ambitious program for an in-house innovation center. Allocating an out-of-use, windowless room for the project, they painted some catchy quotes on the white walls, scattered bean bag chairs across the floor, and set up whiteboards. After this sparse decorating attempt, they were ready to begin . . .or so they thought. In reality, it looked like a low-budget day care center, minus the colorful toys. With no windows and ugly fluorescent lights, it was thoroughly depressing! Predictably, less than a year later, the innovation project had been cancelled and the space reassigned. Is this the best that one of our largest, multinational corporations can do? A kindergarten classroom in the local elementary school could have produced more creative thinking! If some colorful playthings and a few Dr. Seuss books can do wonders in stirring a child's imagination, why not engage adults through the catalyst of a creative and unconventional setting, designed expressly for the clever business of outside-the-box thinking and upending established paradigms!

Everyone will benefit from an interesting and appealing workplace, but for Giraffes, such an atmosphere is critical – a matter of 'cognitive' life and death. Confined in a utilitarian cubicle or private office, short on sunlight, isolated from outside marketplace intelligence, and deprived of sufficient resources, Giraffes will undoubtedly become discouraged and either leave or just stop innovating. Remember, nature's giraffes roam in *loose* herds. Like their counterparts, organizational Giraffes require both mental and physical space!

In 1972, the UNCF, an organization which helps over 60,000 students attend college every year, adopted the following slogan: *A mind is a terrible thing to waste.* This is every bit as true today as it was then, and to waste the mental powers of your organization's Giraffes would be one of the costliest mistakes you could ever make.

If your organization is fortunate enough to be building new facilities, you have a singular opportunity to plan an environment which promotes creativity. Acuity Insurance accomplished this superbly when they constructed their new corporate headquarters in 2004. With an expansive glass atrium design extending the entire length of the building, the structure includes several casual sitting and gathering areas on an open-air second floor balcony. Seven gigantic hand-blown glass chandeliers hang from a vaulted ceiling. The effect is awesome! The building is so remarkable that it became the subject of a Public Television Corporation documentary. Its spectacular design not only enhances Acuity's public image, but transforms the headquarters from one of mere function to art — inspiring surroundings for creative ideation and innovative problem solving!

In 2011, Apple announced their plan to build a new corporate facility in Cupertino, California, just a few miles from the existing one. This campus will have only one primary office building designed to accommodate over 12,000 employees. It will be circular with a beautiful park at the center. In fact, the entire campus will be one large park featuring an 80/20 green space to building footprint, with most of the automobile parking hidden underground. The concept designs of this facility bring to mind a four-story circular flying saucer. And when I use the term circular, I do not mean the typical architectural practice of straight, walled sections, connected at a slight angle to give the impression of being round. It will be an engineering wonder for all to enjoy with 'not a straight piece of glass in the building,' as Steve Jobs promised. Why not take the conventional method of creating merely the illusion of roundness at a far lower cost? Because at Apple, what is worth doing is worth doing right! In their large metropolitan city center stores, they pioneered new technologies for building all glass-fronted facades. Now, they will use those same glass production technologies to create the largest and most magnificent curved glass panels the world has ever seen.

But it doesn't take a new office campus and millions of dollars to generate a positive outcome. An engaging environment can be achieved with very little expense. Start small. Pick an area in the building, perhaps a corridor which people pass through without 'a second thought' everyday or maybe a well-used conference room. One with a glass panel wall would be perfect so that everyone will notice the change. At Zappos, a rising star in online retailing, every glass-walled conference room features a unique theme. Although Zappos' corporate offices are located in Las Vegas, one of their conference rooms has a trendy New York City theme. Rather than hire a designer, the eye-catching themes are selected and developed by employees. At Apple, the conference rooms are named Da Vinci, Picasso, Michelangelo...a lot more exciting than the usual #101 or C-287A.

Be unconventional! Have some fun. You might consider visual stimulation such as multicolored kites, fanciful balloons, photography, pop art, avant-garde art or even zentangle – a kind of doodle art employing structured patterns. Add to this imaginative lighting and image projection. And sound should not be overlooked, for it evokes all kinds of thoughts and feelings. Is there a heavily travelled passageway in your building? Why not install a sound generator? Then let your imagination run wild. Sound offers many possibilities: background music, white noise, or a resonance of nature. In the morning, employees could be greeted with sounds of the jungle. By afternoon, the doldrums could be chased away by a jolting thunderclap and the portentous rumblings of an approaching storm. Or why not restore and revive with the undulating sound of Pacific waves crashing on the shore... and the cry of seagulls, all in a corridor or passageway? This may quickly become the most well travelled corridor in your building.

And we should not forget the sense of smell and its enormous power of suggestion. Think of the memories awakened by a pinewoods scent, cinnamon and cloves, balsam fir or the irresistible fragrance of lilacs in springtime. After all, the mind is refreshed and energized when all of the senses are stimulated. Aromas can arouse many emotions. Almost everything has an odor, whether good or bad. The real issue is whether it evokes a positive or negative human response. Offices are typically neutral, although operations areas may emit disagreeable smells. Enter the world of commercial and industrial automated smart scent defusers. Retailers are now using them to infuse specific store areas with targeted scents, which are always detectable to customers and have a positive effect on buying behavior.

If you have ever sold a home, you may have heard of the tried and true realtor's advice about making a batch of chocolate chip cookies just before the prospective buyer arrives. Or you may have been advised to set out a vanilla candle diffuser. Such advice has now gone scientific and high tech for business applications. For example, grocery stores are employing scent diffusing systems to calm shoppers waiting in long checkout lines just before the dinner hour. Prolitec Inc. has emerged as an industry leader in supplying sophisticated turn-key scenting services which employ their patented, computer-controlled dispensing systems as well as a wide range of scents for theme enhancement, odor remediation and theme scenting. Applications include:

- Offices

- Factories

- Hotels, airports, and other public buildings

- Malls

- Spas and fitness centers

- Theaters

- Point of sale

- Elevators

- Rest rooms

- Hospitals

- Assisted living facilities

  ...and many other venues.

Anything that refreshes and stimulates mental energies is your goal. And remember, it is not only conscious thought that you are targeting, but also the subliminal. To rekindle the 'flame' of innovation, everything which affects the senses matters. Whatever forms of mental stimulation you choose to implement should be carefully integrated. How will you meet this challenge and inspire your people, especially Giraffes, to achieve new and greater dimensions of performance?

How do you keep a Giraffe happy? What do Giraffes need? For one thing, they need a periodic change of pace, which will also benefit everyone in the organization. Disrupting the workflow now and then will uplift morale and serve to boost overall productivity. While teaching an innovation seminar, I suggested occasionally arranging an unannounced 'disruptive moment,' such as bringing in live entertainment – a mariachi band, for example. Immediately, one attendee raised an objection because the people in his office were usually on the phone. Therefore, 'such an outlandish idea could not be considered.' One woman shot back that only the month before her employer had done just that. Musicians strolled through the office with huge smiles and trumpets blaring! She went on to say that at that very moment, she was on the phone with a customer, so she politely asked the customer if she could call her back shortly. When she did, the customer wanted to know what all the commotion was about. She explained that it was surprise entertainment, something her company periodically arranged for the employees just for fun. The customer remarked that, she wished she had an employer who cared that much! Such brief but lively interruptions do much to build morale and community. Another morale and creativity booster is to bring in a team of masseuses to give your employees five minute neck massages. This is common in large airports, why not at the office where tension frequently runs high? Take a small risk, try something new . . . then watch the benefits accrue.

Your customers and suppliers will understand. Once they discover that you regularly invest in your employees in these small but powerful ways to break up their day and add enjoyment, you may become the talk of your industry! Mankind may have to earn its living by the sweat of the brow, but a little diversion will lighten the load and spread some much needed sunshine

Hard work can still be *fun*! It has been repeatedly proven that happy people are more productive, yet it sometimes seems as though happiness is a punishable offense in many of today's organizations.

As employers, we only hurt ourselves when we become arbitrary. When good people are not given room to navigate, we cramp their style. Micromanagement results in lower productivity, not to mention a great deal of frustration and misunderstanding! Could the same people achieve greater potential if we would only loosen up? Yes, they might fail – but even if they do fail, something learned is something gained. On the other hand, you may discover that your people have many hidden talents. **People will always be your greatest resource.** Our organizations become far more productive when leadership and management teams manage by being in command, but not constantly in control.

For decades, IBM required all of their sales and management personnel to wear dark blue suits. This policy has since been abandoned. It may have promoted an image of uniformity and professionalism, but did nothing to foster outside-the-box thinking. IBM did not understand the value in questioning and asking, 'Why do we...?' In the meantime, they were passed up by competitors with more imaginative paradigms.

Many forms of mental stimulation can be quite simply achieved. Why not give cafeterias, lunch rooms and break rooms a facelift? Try painting the walls in vivid colors, rearranging furniture frequently and choosing zesty motifs. Every office facility should include informal meeting and working areas with couches and other comfortable furniture.   Equip these areas with familiar reading materials along with thought-provoking publications. In addition to favorites like *People, Sports Illustrated,* and *Vogue,* expand the selection with more creative and intellectually stimulating magazines, for example: *Architectural Digest, Fast Company, Australian Geographic, Country Living, Popular Science, Popular Mechanics, Where, Decor, Budget Travel, Coastal Living, American Cinematographer, American Photo, Better Homes and Gardens, American History, Architectural Digest, Air & Space, American Scientist, Art...* Your actual choice of publications is less important than supplying a wide variety, especially for the Giraffes. Illustrated coffee table books highlighting interesting subjects and destinations can also be scattered about, as well as humorous books such as *A Fool and His Bunny, A Couple of Longnecks, Hare of the Dog,* and *a fool moon* by author and artist Will Bullas. These are a great starting point.   Keep the selection current and always continue adding to your collection, rotating these materials frequently.

Think about adding puzzles and some games – such as chess, checkers, or nerf basketball – to the break room. You may be thinking, 'What if employees become involved in a chess game and spend hours playing'? They won't. Not if they are responsible. Encourage 'open games,' where the board sits out and anyone who happens by can make the next move. A company owner I know recently installed an in-office basketball hoop and ping pong table. His concern for his employees is more than apparent. Consequently, his employees are very motivated. Investing in your people builds morale and loyalty.

Depending on how many gathering places you have, consider allocating an initial $200 to each and then $50 per calendar quarter to keep refreshing the supply of magazines, books, and games. This is a minimal investment, but it will give your people a welcome respite from the daily routine and provide fuel for resetting the mind, igniting the imagination and triggering innovation.

When water is readily available, wild giraffes drink up to twelve gallons a day. However, they can go several days without drinking, hydrating through the foliage they eat. Organizational Giraffes hydrate by browsing for ideas and scoping out the competition as well as other industries to learn what people are thinking, seeking new concepts from outside of the organization. Without a steady flow of new information, their idea generating capacity shrivels.

Exposure not only to what is new and unusual, but more fundamentally, evaluating the *different* is critical. The opportunity to refresh and refuel by gaining new perspectives and experiences allows Giraffes to regularly recharge their mental energies.

Authors can't write, artists can't paint, and Giraffes can't ideate without having the time to reflect. Giraffes often require a change of scene. Some of my best and most complex problem solving ideas have been generated while walking through a store, sitting on a beach or relaxing in a boat and not consciously focused on work issues. Do you remember the experience of James Watts related in Chapter Five? He was the Scotsman who invented the first rotary-motion steam engine in 1781. Watts was simply taking a walk when the idea came to him.

On an afternoon in 1941, a Swiss engineer named Georges de Mestral also went for a walk with his dog in an alpine woods. Anyone who is an outdoorsman can identify with the aggravating experience of realizing upon his return that they were both covered with burrs. Sitting down to begin picking the burrs off himself and the dog before entering the house, Mestral was struck by a *thought*. Could there possibly be a positive use for something that could stick to most surfaces and yet be easily detached and reattached as needed?

After eight years of researching the idea, Mestral was able devise a workable pair of cloth strips, one covered with loops and the other with little hooks. The result, VELCRO! He patented his invention in 1955. Shortly thereafter, he improved it by using the far more durable nylon instead of the cotton.

The product was nicknamed the zipperless zipper and in the 1960s gained worldwide attention when NASA astronauts utilized it to prevent pens and other objects from drifting around in the weightlessness of their space capsule. Once innovative product designers recognized the simplicity and economy of the little nylon strips, it didn't take long for the Velcro market to explode. Today its applications have become so universal that it is essentially a part of our vocabulary.

Once again, an inquisitive mind addressing a small inconvenience (problem) of daily life, opened the way to the creation of a multi-billion dollar industry. Maybe you should be sending your Giraffe innovators out in the real world on walks more often.

Like a bolt of lightening, an idea will suddenly flash into a Giraffe's head — seemingly out of nowhere. Actually, it was there all along, subconsciously at work, being turned over and over in the mind as the Giraffe continued ruminating in search of a breakthrough. It is no wonder that Giraffes sometimes have a far away look. They may be looking right at you, but only be half-there. They are *thinking*. Have patience, your Giraffe may be solving a very important problem.

Did you ever wonder how a giraffe sleeps? It would be pretty difficult for them to curl up into a ball. Amazingly, their necks make an arch over their backs. They rest their heads on their hind legs and usually remain standing. Wild giraffes don't require much sleep. In fact, they will sleep less than two hours (in five to fifteen minute intervals) in the course of twenty-four hours. The bottom line is that they browse much and sleep little.

Like their counterparts, human Giraffes rarely rest...at least from the mental activity of ideation and problem solving. It is continuous, on and off the job. This is why they require a constant flow of new information. They also need change at regular intervals. This could involve investigating cutting-edge technology either inside or outside your industry, scenic vistas for reflection, traveling to new places to meet people, discovering what is new, absorbing anything and everything that could change the paradigm and reveal an opportunity for Giraffes to do their magic. Change is the much needed hydration of Giraffes.

Community is also key in establishing a support structure that enables Giraffes to accomplish their innovation objectives. Giraffes prefer to work in groups, but they also require the assistance of detail-oriented staff who can provide the functional support needed to keep them organized. They enjoy company and flourish when they can volley ideas back and forth with team members, especially other Giraffes. In Proverbs, it says, *As iron sharpens iron, one mind sharpens another.* While ideation may occur on an individual basis, the threshing out and ongoing development of innovative ideas proceeds much faster in a group setting where everyone involved is on the same page. Collaboration allows the spark of an idea to be fanned into the flame of a market-changing breakthrough in an accelerated timeframe. When innovation teams collaborate effectively, the results can be phenomenal.

To keep the Giraffes in your organization 'on the reserve,' their needs must be carefully addressed. Granted, they are peculiar, outside-the-box personalities differing vastly from the majority. The purpose of this book is to help you identify Giraffe innovators, cultivate a corporate culture of innovation and achieve continuous innovation breakthroughs. To do this, it is necessary to understand who Giraffes are and how they function. Then you will know how to support them in creating essential innovations. If you don't have any Giraffes, then you are in peril and need to hunt some down. Once the Giraffes are in place, you can turn your attention to securing optimal conditions for an environment which encourages and supports their ingenuity.

The organizational directives your leadership team initiates for the benefit of Giraffes will prove a windfall for other employees. A revamped and upbeat environment offering the expanded freedoms (though perhaps greater demands and challenges) of living with Giraffes can be thrilling. The very idea of participating in the development of real innovation and having unprecedented opportunities to learn and excel will inspire your employees. The resulting teamwork will ignite a sense of shared purpose throughout your organization.

So why do we go to so much trouble to feed, water, and otherwise sustain these unusual characters? Because, Giraffes possess an uncanny aptitude for seeing and identifying breakthrough opportunities others do not.

1. Giraffes are visionaries. They see the big picture.

2. Giraffes have ideas. They create opportunities through the power of innovation.

3. As complex problem solvers, Giraffes will relentlessly tackle problems until optimal solutions are found.

4. Giraffes abandon established thinking patterns and reject all limitations. They will defy the impossible to successfully realize innovations.

It is true, they can be frequently misunderstood and are not always easy to live with, but Giraffes are the ultimate innovators. If you are looking for miracles, keep them home and contented on the reserve.

Giraffe Example:

Santiago Calatrava

[Architecture is] the greatest of all the arts because it embraces the others - music, painting, sculpture. I couldn't be an architect without doing those things.

Santiago Calatrava is a master artist and licensed architect and engineer, a designer, and sculptor. He obtained his undergraduate architecture degree as well as a post-graduate degree in urbanism at the Polytechnic University of Valencia, Spain. During this period, he and a group of fellow students produced two books on the regional architecture of Valencia and Ibiza.

After graduating in 1975, Calatrava realized that his training as an architect would place him in the position of needing to work with engineers in order to ensure that his designs were translated into plans that were structurally sound. Well aware of the tension that often arises between architects and engineers, he decided to avoid the issue altogether by enrolling in the Swiss Federal Institute of Technology in Zurich, Switzerland, where he earned a PhD in Civil Engineering.

His professional career began in 1981, with a principal focus on designing train stations and bridges. In so doing, he demonstrated elegance in melding design with functionality. His brilliantly fluid designs reflect an intensive study of the human body, as well as the natural world surrounding his creations. His celebrated projects have included such notable structures as the 80th Street Residential Skyscraper, the New World Trade Center Transportation Hub, the Trinity River Bridges in Dallas, the pedestrian Peace Bridge in Calgary, the new campus of the University of South Florida Polytechnic, and the Milwaukee Art Museum addition.

Calatrava's structures synthesize new technologies with new forms. His original designs transcend the traditional boundaries between art, architecture, and engineering. His many projects have won him critical acclaim internationally. The innovative architecture of a Calatrava project can be described as both beautiful and awe-inspiring.

Chapter 7 — Thought Questions

1. Does our organization have an established method of rewarding Giraffe innovators in order to keep them?

2. How do we rate our office decor in terms of inspiring creativity and ideation?

3. What are quick and inexpensive actions our organization could take to test the merits of refreshing our office environment to make it more creative?

4. What elements do I think would be important to incorporate into an office refresh, i.e., color, graphics, plants, lighting, sounds, scents, etc.?

5. What do I think of Apple's attitude that, *What is worth doing is worth doing right!*

6. How would our organization respond to the suggestion of orchestrating 'disruptive moments' periodically?

7. Why is exposure to what is 'different' so important to Giraffes?

8. Why is getting out and 'taking a walk' so powerful for Giraffe innovators?

9. Does our organization presently have any Giraffes? If so, in what capacities? Are they recognized formally and functioning as Giraffe innovators?

10. If we currently have one or more Giraffes onboard, who is responsible for ensuring that they obtain the needed variety of experiences so that they can remain fresh and creative?

11. What is the most important contribution a Giraffe could make to our organization right now?

12. Why is Santiago Calatrava's architecture so celebrated around the world, across different nationalities and cultures?

Leadership ultimately determines how innovative organizations will become.

Chapter Eight: When the Giraffes Lead

Nature's giraffes have what could only be described as supercharged hearts! They possess a very efficient cardiovascular system with special valves to regulate the blood supply. Because of their long necks, the resulting hydrostatic pressure exerted on the heart is extremely high. Their hearts must be very powerful to overcome the downward pull of gravity. Giraffes have double the blood pressure of a human being, with their hearts beating twice as fast — 170 times a minute. A very thick left ventricle wall provides the needed muscle to pump blood all that long way up to the brain.

A Giraffe innovator's heart beats for innovation. It is their passion and their goal. While Giraffes have a heart for innovation, there are often many hurdles to overcome. What happens when Giraffes lead? Depending on his or her leadership skill set, it can portend the very best of times or, indeed, the worst! Giraffes typically lead small start-up companies, especially in the tech, bio and other cutting-edge industries. Over time and with success, the Founder/CEO Giraffe will either evolve into a more traditional, management-oriented executive or else recruit a CEO or COO to run operations so that, unfettered, the Giraffe may continue pursuing the kind of breakthrough innovations which first created the enterprise. There are exceptions to this model, the most notable being the co-founders of Apple, Steve Jobs and Steve Wozniak.

While still in their teens, Jobs and Wozniak met and joined forces to become the perfect team. They became friends in 1970, when Jobs (14 at the time) worked a summer job at Hewlett-Packard where Wozniak (then 19) was working on the mainframe computer. Woz was a technical genius. As their friendship grew, they became involved with the *Homebrew Computer Club*, in Menlo Park, California. Jobs had the idea to sell a personal computer as a fully assembled circuit board. Wozniak was skeptical, but agreed to collaborate. They sold some of their possessions (Wozniak's HP calculator and Jobs' VW van) and were able to raise $1,300 to finance the assembly of the first prototype in Job's bedroom and then, when they ran out of space, in the garage. Both of them were Giraffes, but with clearly different orientations. Jobs was the highly conceptual, big picture, strategic innovator and marketer par excellence — while Wozniak supplied the practical, more technically focused, down to earth, 'make it happen in real time' innovations. Each needed the other. Both were Giraffes. Together, they proved unstoppable.

Steve Wozniak is undoubtedly the first person to conceive of a computer mouse. One day, he caught a live mouse in the Apple offices and put it inside Dick Huston's, Apple's Senior Engineer, Apple II computer as a prank (Apple's culture encouraged having fun) and noted that Dick 'looked pretty puzzled at the noises it made.' Little did Wozniak realize that this incident marked the beginning of a lifelong love affair with 'mice.'

Jobs was a master at ideating with other Giraffes. Dean Hovey, a Stanford graduate and one of the founding partners of the emerging industrial design firm Hovey-Kelley Design, relates how one day in 1980, he arranged a meeting with Steve Jobs. Hovey's firm had been making component parts for Apple, but they were looking for greater involvement. They wanted to move into designing complete products. As their lunch meeting began, Hovey had no sooner begun to pitch his ideas when Jobs stopped him cold. 'Stop, Dean,' Hovey recalled Jobs telling him. 'What you guys need to do, what we need to do together, is build a mouse.' But what was a mouse?

Jobs described, literally on a napkin, the intriguing concept of a small, hand-operated, pointing device that could control a computer without a keyboard. Jobs had just visited Xerox Parc, the R&D center for Xerox Corporation. There he encountered 'Star,' a futuristic computer workstation, still in development that incorporated the first ever Graphical User Interface (GUI), an innovation soon to replace the standard green dot prompt screen of early computers. While there, Jobs had seen a crude hand-pointing device which set his imagination spinning. This innovation was destined to become a household word — the ubiquitous 'mouse.'

The computer mouse has an eclectic history. Although similar devices had been previously suggested, it was not until 1965 that Bill English, while working at SRI (Stanford Research Institute) published an article detailing the 'Computer-Aided Display Control' in which he first coined the term 'mouse.' Three years later, the German company Telefunken published an article about a device they called the 'Rollkugel' ('rolling ball' in English). However, it was not until the early 1980's, with the advent of the 'Lisa' and 'Mac' computers, when Apple introduced the first GUI Interface computers that the 'mouse' emerged as a global phenomenon.

Hovey's meeting with Job's had whetted his appetite. On his way back to the office, he stopped at what he jokingly referred to as the 'mouse parts store'— the Palo Alto Walgreens. There he acquired the critical ingredients for his experiment: balls that could be used as rollers and a housing. The balls came from various sized bottles of roll-on deodorant with a plastic butter dish cover for the housing. Over the weekend, he 'hacked together' the first conceptual prototype. But later, as more components were required, his wife discovered one morning that the reason their refrigerator no longer worked was because parts had been 'requisitioned for the cause.' When the need arose, Hovey's business partner, David Kelley, temporarily sacrificed the stick shift ball from his BMW. Jim Sachs, another founding member of Hovey-Kelley recalled, 'We all did the same thing, we sacrificed circuitry, we sacrificed anything. The idea of [formally] designing something and having everything fabricated to your specifications was simply too long, slow and expensive.

[Better to] take apart something else, or find something similar, and glue it together or cut it in half.'

Such was the drive of this young team of design engineers whom Jobs had inspired. But what was this task which was so 'undoable,' and required such dedication? After all, hadn't Xerox Parc already developed a working mouse prototype? More or less. According to Alex Soojung-Kim Pang, in an article which appeared in *Stanford Magazine*:

> A commercial mouse based on the Xerox technology cost $400, malfunctioned regularly and was nearly impossible to clean. That device — a descendant of the original computer mouse invented by Douglas Englebart at the Stanford Research Institute in the early 1960s — was a masterpiece of high-concept technology, but a hopeless product. Jobs wanted a mouse that could be manufactured for $10 to $35, survive everyday use and work on his jeans. 'We thought maybe Steve wasn't getting enough meat in his diet,' says Jim Sachs, also of Hovey-Kelley Design, 'but for $25 an hour, we'd design a solar-powered toaster if that's what he wanted.'

The toaster probably would have been easier. Jobs wanted Hovey-Kelley to take a piece of technology developed by some of Silicon Valley's greatest minds, dramatically improve its reliability and cut its price by more than 90 percent. Hovey continued, 'When you're in one of those modes where you're building something and you need a part, you figure, either I can stop and wait, or I can go forward and wreck [the refrigerator]. But it'll be $20 to fix it — it's no big deal. When you're in the midst of the passion of designing, you just do it.'

Never underestimate a Giraffe running at full gallop
with an extraordinary idea.

Giraffes can become an effective creative force at all levels of the organization. One idea alone can revolutionize an industry. However, for Giraffes to succeed as CEOs, they must also possess strong leadership ability. For example, with each new growth phase an organization achieves, difficult transitions need to be made. However, when a Giraffe company founder fails to adapt to his or her changing role, problems ensue.

Leadership ultimately determines how innovative an organization will become. A familiar adage affirms that: '*The speed of the leader determines the rate of the pack.*' This maxim is universal and probably ought to be engraved on the walls of every organization – whether corporate, government or philanthropic. People cannot outstrip their leadership, and if they attempt to do so, they end up either pulling back or simply leaving the organization out of frustration. Most people are not leaders. In fact, too many leaders can be worse than too few. We need sea captains and sailors — and far more sailors than sea captains or ships would never leave port. But my point is that if you own a company, but are not comfortable leading it, then find someone who can. Do yourself and your people a favor; let go of the reins. Free yourself to do what you do best, return to being a Giraffe innovator.

Excellent leadership is crucial to the progress and productivity of any organization. People need and want strong, decisive leaders who they can follow with confidence! Today, the role of leadership is largely misunderstood. Unfortunately, the function of management is often mistakenly equated with leadership. These are two discrete functions and should never be confused. In fact, it is really not appropriate to apply the word 'management' to people at all. To be precise:

We should lead people and manage things.

For organizations to be successful over the long term, people need an effective combination of visionary leaders and Giraffe innovators. If Giraffes possess leadership skills and have the sense to recognize their limitations, it is entirely possible for them to function as visionary executive leaders. Perhaps, the most prominent, contemporary examples of successful Giraffe leadership are Steve Jobs and Steve Wozniak who recognized they needed not only the complement of each other's abilities, but a growing cadre of highly creative, dedicated and excited people to turn their vision into reality.

Things do not go well when Giraffe leaders fail to understand or accept that, regardless of how brilliant and charismatic they may be, they must delegate responsibilities to others. No one person can successfully master every aspect of a growing enterprise. The demands of daily operations alone can be draining, allowing little remaining time for strategic thinking, creativity, ideation and innovation.

When an organization is capably led by Giraffes, the effect can be synergistic. As visionaries, they have the ability to recognize and strategically assess the possibilities, the perception to create an atmosphere for encouraging innovation and the passion to instill a sense of fulfillment and purpose for empowering innovation. At Apple, Jobs stated, 'What we're doing here will send a giant ripple through the universe.' He believed in the validity and significance of his vision, that the personal computer would level the playing field, enabling anyone to do *real work productively*. He challenged coworkers by insisting, 'What you can imagine can get made.'

Giraffe leaders demonstrating such profound vision and determination will excite and motivate their people as few others can. Jobs understood that product design is a creative enterprise that cannot be regimented. Rather, it can only be successfully achieved by small, mutually accountable, cohesive teams dreaming up new product ideas. He ensured that his teams received the vital support needed to develop those innovations. Aside from frequent design reviews and being answerable to real world time and price constraints, design team members were allowed the freedom to work outside of conventional structures. While Jobs made heavy demands, he gave Giraffes room to maneuver, because he understood exactly how creative minds work.

After tracking down outstanding creative talent, Jobs made every effort to keep them happy and productive. He was always thinking up ways to express appreciation, generously rewarding individuals for their achievements. People were important to Jobs because it was his firm belief that it takes great people to design great products.

Under Jobs, Apple functioned as an organism, in contrast to the typical siloed organization. It fostered a culture of unconventional leadership, which rewarded on the merits of ingenuity, passion and performance. Believing their personal investment was appreciated and valued, employees came to respect Jobs' leadership. He always had a new idea. On the day of the initial Mac rollout, in an astonishing gesture, he arranged for semitrailer loads of Mac computers to be delivered to Apple headquarters and distributed to every Apple employee – including part timers and contractors – to express his sincere appreciation for all of their efforts. Apple employees willingly strove to meet nearly impossible standards of performance in order to be the 'best.' The priority at Apple was never really about making money or self-interest, but about a vision of excellence which Jobs and Wozniak instilled into every Apple employee. Apple became an organism, a thriving community of highly motivated, interconnected individuals, discovering 'what is possible' and continuously innovating to create better products.

In some ways, visionary leaders are like legendary commanding generals who led dedicated armies into battle and, after crossing their Rubicons, had the courage to burn bridges behind them. Organizations with a 'sold out' commitment to be the 'best' and a mindset of no retreat will exceed all expectations to achieve extraordinary outcomes. That is the hallmark of excellent leadership.

Giraffes are rarely found at the top of larger organizations. Increasingly, however, forward-thinking companies are creating new, senior level positions, such as Chief Innovation Officer (CIO) and Chief Strategic Officer (CSO). This places a Giraffe, or at least someone who ought to be one, at the most senior and influential level of the organization. Merging the organization's creative 'vision' with the leadership empowerment and oversight of products, services, processes and systems development provides the necessary clout to expedite and implement strategic innovations. Additionally, this assures the 'ear' of other members of the senior executive team, enabling the CIO/CSO Giraffe to rally support in promoting a culture of creativity, ideation and innovation across the entire organization.

Wherever Giraffes are found in your organization, they need the authority, moral support, and necessary resources to be effective. This includes ready access to anyone and anything holding the key to realizing their innovations. Traditional corporations can be a virtual graveyard for innovative ideas. Xerox PARC did initially develop the GUI Interface and (together with SRI) the computer mouse, but it was Apple that made the combination a blockbuster, market-changing reality.

Kodak executives sat by as the digital market emerged, tightly managing costs (lean thinking) and reducing company headcount to improve short term profitability. In the mid-1970s, Kodak joined the digital camera age as its scientists invented several solid-state image sensors that successfully 'converted light into digital pictures' for professional and retail consumer use. Then in 1986, Kodak scientists invented the world's first megapixel sensor, the brain of all digital cameras. Even though they already had the scientific capability and brand equity to dominate the market, Kodak fell victim to the classic error of aggressively pursuing major cost-savings concurrently with innovation. Innovation took a back seat. Consequently, the strongest and most consistent message pervading the organization was to avoid the risk taking necessary for strategic innovation. Instead, play it safe, be risk-averse and protect your job was the unofficial, but clear message conveyed. Managers and employees were justifiably fearful about the consequences of failure and therefore, believed it was safer to continue doing what they had always done, maintaining the Kodak status quo — film. Kodak's executive leaders failed to grasp the vision that film was dying and the digital age of photography was at hand.

Such behavior inevitably creates a self-fulfilling cycle. If the organization does not create an environment where people can take risks and fail, then innovation will be stifled. If innovation doesn't occur, the company will not experience profitable growth and will be compelled to continue 'making its numbers' through ever deepening cost-cutting. This intensifies the environment of fear, further reducing any chance of innovation and triggering a menacing downward spiral.

It is generally far more difficult for a large organization to bring truly innovative ideas successfully to the marketplace, because of all the internal 'barbed wire and barricades.' And, if you want to hold onto your highly-talented junior Giraffes, not presently in positions of leadership, you must ensure that their innovations have a fighting chance of being realized. Giraffes can make great strides only when leadership advocates and supports their efforts. With the help of key innovators in high profile positions, as well as the executive support of a Chief Innovation Officer, Giraffes throughout the organization will be readily accepted as development team leaders.

Leadership is all about gaining followers. You aren't a leader if you don't have followers. And for Giraffe innovators, adherents are crucial since the nature of their mandate will likely cut across all organizational lines. When a culture of innovation is systemic, participants may not always be under the Giraffe's direct authority, unless that Giraffe happens to be the CEO. Yet, they may be expected and held accountable for following their lead in supporting development and implementation.

Innovators create extraordinary opportunities for dynamic growth and profitability because they think beyond perceived limitations. They envision *what is possible*. Giraffe innovators find creative solutions to complex problems. They inspire a culture of innovation. When Giraffes lead well, breakthrough innovations follow. When effective leaders, who are not themselves Giraffe innovators, empower Giraffes to spearhead innovation, good things also follow.

Giraffe Example:

William Pitt the Younger

Necessity is the plea for every infringement of human freedom. It is the argument of tyrants; it is the creed of slaves.

In 1783, at the age of only twenty-four, William Pitt the Younger became the youngest ever Prime Minister of Great Britain. (His father had also served as Prime Minister before him.) Pitt the Younger held office twice: first from 1783 to 1801 and then from 1804 until his death in 1806. Immediately after becoming the new Prime Minister in 1783, he was defeated in Parliament by a vote of *No Confidence*, but refused to resign. In 1784, Parliament was dissolved for a general election, which Pitt won.

As a boy, Pitt was weak and sickly, so his parents had him home-schooled by the Reverend Edward Wilson, a graduate of Cambridge University. By the age of seven he was proficient in Latin. His father set his sights on his son becoming an excellent orator and would listen to the boy's recitations from Greek and Latin rhetoricians. In 1773, at the age of fourteen, Pitt entered Pembroke Hall, which is now Cambridge University. There he received a classical education, studying English history, political philosophy and mathematics. He graduated in 1776.

Pitt strongly opposed the prevailing system of partisan politics and institutional corruption within the current government, a stance for which he gained the popular title of 'Honesty Bill.' He also favored legislation to abolish slavery throughout the British Empire. Indeed, he encouraged and collaborated with his close friend William Wilberforce to set the stage for passage of the landmark Slave Trade Act of 1807, which signified an official end to the slave trade in the British Empire. Britain became the only nation to station navy squadrons off the west coast of Africa to intercept slave ships.

Immediately following the American War of Independence (or the 'Rebellion,' from the British viewpoint) there existed in Parliament a widely held view that the loss of the American colonies would prove catastrophic to Great Britain's economy. However, economist Adam Smith argued that Britain could actually *gain* more economically from increased trade with the newly independent nation than it had previously achieved through unsuccessful attempts to tax the colonies and limit their industrial development. Pitt adopted this more modern economic mindset espoused by Smith.

A closely related prevailing viewpoint of the era had been that military conquest and expansion of an empire was the key to gaining financial control over new supplies of natural resources to be acquired for processing by the 'home' nation's industries. The resulting products could then be re-exported as finished goods throughout the empire. The new and contrasting theory held that increasing trade depended instead upon independent countries becoming expanding trade partners. This new perspective, which Pitt fully embraced and championed, resulted in an immense upsurge in British industrial production and trade following America's independence. It actually rescued England from the weight of its immense debts, including those incurred in its unsuccessful war with the American colonies.

The 2008 banking debacle (the banking mortgage derivative scandal) is reminiscent of a similar economic crisis faced by Pitt as Prime Minister more than 200 years ago. At the time, Bank Notes brought to the Bank of England could be exchanged for gold or silver. (This was also the original currency plan in the US. However, in 1933, gold and silver backing for currency was abolished by federal law under the Franklin Delano Roosevelt administration.) In 1797, a crisis of confidence erupted and spread like contagion throughout the financial markets. Traders began exchanging their Notes in a run on the official Bank of England. To solve this crisis, the Pitt government worked in cooperation with the Bank to devise innovative financial measures that stemmed the mounting panic. One of these innovations included introducing £2 and £5 paper Notes for the first time. The new measures helped to restore confidence and, with paper money now available to satisfy traders, they no longer felt the need to convert their funds.

In 1785, rejecting the protectionism that had characterized the mercantile economics of the past, Pitt sought to bring Ireland into a commercial free-trade union with Britain. In 1786, he negotiated a treaty with France, establishing unhindered access for both countries to one another's ports as well as enacting low tariff rates, thereby encouraging greatly expanded trade.

Pitt also simplified the British tax code, introducing new taxes (such as a temporary 10% income tax over a base income of £200 per year) in 1799, in order to fund yet another war with France while simultaneously reducing other taxes across the board. He also took action to curtail the rampant smuggling enterprises that evaded taxes. Additionally, Pitt modernized the Exchequer (Treasury Department). Until that time, revenue from taxes and outflows from government expenditures had been segregated into numerous separate funds. These he streamlined into one 'consolidated fund,' thus adding transparency to the government's finances. The system which Pitt introduced remains in effect to this day. In 1786, Pitt also established a £1 million annual 'sinking fund' for the exclusive purpose of paying off any future national debt that might accumulate due to wars or other unforeseen events.

Although Pitt was an eighteenth-century Tory and a loyal supporter of King George III, he never forgot the 'common man' and fought hard to make government responsive to the general welfare of all citizens. In 1801, after opposing the king by supporting a bill to repeal laws in Ireland that restricted Catholics from openly practicing their faith, Pitt was forced from office. However, in 1804, with the resumption of the British war with France, the king was forced to have Pitt reinstated as Prime Minister.

Pitt was not only the youngest Prime Minister in British history, he was also one of the most innovative. His economic, banking and political reforms for the benefit of society, together with his staunch support for the efforts of his close friend William Wilberforce in his lifelong fight to abolish slavery and the slave trade, earned him a place of lasting distinction in British history.

Chapter 8 — Thought Questions

1. Do you agree that, *Leadership ultimately determines how innovative organizations will become*?

2. Have you ever experienced working in an organization where Giraffes led? What was it like?

3. Can you relate to the Hovey-Kelley Design team's willingness to sacrifice components from other projects and even personal items to help move their 'mouse' project for Apple along faster?

4. Would our innovation teams think it usual to leave a meeting and stop by an 'innovation parts store,' such as a Walgreens, Target, Home Depot or Dollar Store to scavenge parts for experimentation or prototyping?

5. How would our organization relate to cutting things in half, glueing things together and other unorthodox methods of pushing the rate of product development instead of the traditional practice of designing each discrete component for prototyping?

6. What would we think of a design requirement that cut the cost by 90%, required the product to be durable, elegant, simple to use and able to be operated on one's jeans?

7. What are creative ways our organization could reward Giraffe innovators, teams and the entire organization when a highly successful innovation becomes a reality?

8. What are the differences between organizations that operate as an organism versus siloed?

9. What would be the potential dangers or benefits of 'burning the bridges' behind us when creating critical innovations?

10. Must one burn the bridges to become an organization with, *A sold out commitment to be the 'best' and a mindset of no retreat, which will exceed all expectations to achieve extraordinary outcomes*?

11. Why are Giraffe innovators rarely found at the top of large, well established organizations?

12. With its massive resources, why couldn't Xerox PARC successfully commercialize the GUI and the mouse?

13. Does our organization have a CIO or CSO? Should we? What roles could they play in spurring and fostering organization wide innovation?

14. Why do Giraffes need followers?

15. How important to our organization's future sustainability is, *envisioning what is possible*?

16. What besides his youthfulness, made William Pitt, the Younger, so unique as a Prime Minister?

17. What does Pitt's refusal to resign immediately after being becoming Prime Minister, due to a 'No Confidence' vote in Parliament, tell you about his character and how do you think that played out in his role as an innovative Prime Minister?

18. How did embracing Adam Smith's economic principles turn the British economy away from Mercantilism?

Understanding the essential characteristics to look for in a Giraffe places you well ahead of the curve in your search.

Chapter Nine: Finding Your Giraffes

The reticulated giraffe is so named because its coat is covered with a 'network' of patches. The Greeks called the giraffe *camelopardalis*, meaning 'camel marked like a leopard.' The spots are unique to each giraffe, in much the same way fingerprints are unique to each person. The attractive patchwork pattern on their coats serves a very important purpose. It acts as camouflage helping the Giraffe to 'disappear' when danger threatens. However, there is more to this pattern than meets the eye. Underneath each patch lies a sophisticated system of blood vessels – one large blood vessel branching off into smaller ones. Blood travels through these smaller branches into the middle of the patch in order to release heat. Each patch functions as a cooling mechanism, or thermal window, for releasing body heat. Consequently, giraffes can tolerate very hot climates. When the pressure's on, organizational Giraffes must exercise a similar endurance to 'heat.'

Finding your Giraffes is serious business, because continuous breakthrough innovation is the key to the future. In building a culture of innovation you begin with the most capable innovators, Giraffes, and build around them.

There are two places to look for the Giraffes your organization needs — inside and outside. Let's focus first on finding those giraffes that may be already on board. The fastest approach would to be to send another Giraffe 'to sniff' them out. After all, it takes one to know one. Or does it? By now, you should have a very good idea of what a Giraffe looks like and, on looking around, be much better able to identify them. Do not be surprised if you don't find any at first. Depending on a given organization's track record (how receptive and open it has been in the past) it is entirely possible that none have survived.

After years of frustration in striving to have executive leaders, peers, and others recognize what they have been seeing all along – namely, that the seeds of breakthrough opportunities often lie hidden within common problems and everyday circumstances – they may have moved on to more accepting environments, where the culture supports their ideas and efforts. If so, it is unfortunate, but not irreversible. New talent can be imported from other locales where they are thriving.

What is actually a more difficult scenario is flushing out the Giraffes who are still around, but in hiding. They may have become disillusioned, cynical, and so discouraged that they have resorted to camouflage. They may have retreated into an inner world of ideas for innovations that never see the light of day – where their spirits die a little more each day, until one day they stop imagining all together. If this is your predicament, good luck! Resuscitating disaffiliated Giraffes is a formidable task, though not necessarily a lost cause.

To borrow a line from the classic movie, *The Princess Bride*, 'If they are mostly dead, they are still a little bit alive. But if they are all dead, then all you can do is go through their pockets and look for loose change.' Reviving the 'mostly dead' is always a challenge and not without risks; however, in this instance, it is worth the risk!

A word of warning: if you come charging in on your white horse, proclaiming the virtues of innovation, undercover Giraffes will most likely lay back their ears and pull up defenses. Bright and highly creative people who have been banished to the organizational 'outback' for any length of time will understandably be wary of a sudden commitment to innovation.

If there is more than one Giraffe present, they will likely band together in passive resistance. The more the organization's executive leaders call attention to 'innovation,' the more suspicious they will become. They may, inadvertently, be driven even deeper into hiding. Why? Because Giraffes are the primary innovators and they were exiled, precisely because they were proponents of innovation. Now, suddenly, *innovation* becomes a buzzword and the organization's leadership is on board and pushing. The Giraffes will no doubt be skeptical, viewing it as another passing management fad.

It is possible to resurrect 'almost dead' Giraffes, but this will not occur overnight and it will take much more than pep talks from the executive leaders to turn the situation around. It will require meaningful action and a determined effort to rebuild communication and trust with the Giraffes. You may ask if it doesn't make more sense to find new Giraffes and cut the existing ones loose? This is not advisable as, in addition to generating further mistrust, it would create a knowledge deficit. If you still have living, breathing giraffes on the reserve, then you need to make a genuine attempt to restore hope by creating an innovation friendly habitat to which they can return.

Meaningful changes that positively influence the organization's culture speak the loudest. Concrete action demonstrates a long term commitment to place innovation at the core of the organization's values. What do such meaningful steps look like? To begin with, they are not short term. Short term actions, which involve little risk and can easily be reversed or cancelled, will likely be interpreted as taking a 'stab' at innovation. Giraffes may run the other way. Instead, your Giraffes will need to see clear indications of a new reality permeating the organization. Otherwise, why should they 'stick their necks out,' only to risk having them lopped off, should the whims of management suddenly shift once again?

Remember, innovation entails risk and anyone (Giraffes included) who has ever been at the forefront of taking a calculated risk which did not play out as planned, knows that, in most organizations, failures are usually followed up by a witch hunt. Such conduct is antithetical to fostering innovation, as innovation not only requires risk, but involves frequent failures. At Apple, Steve Jobs succeeded in keeping his Giraffes, largely because they felt secure. When things went wrong, he was a good forgiver.

If your organization is not experiencing innovation experiments that regularly *fail*, you are not stretching the boundaries far enough. You are playing it way too safe. Risk is part of the innovation process and cannot be separated from it. A plaque on the wall of my office reads:

'A ship in the harbor is safe, but ships were not meant for the harbor.'

What types of actions will Giraffes interpret as indications of a permanent change in attitude and direction which supports innovation? Here are some suggestions:

- Begin encouraging ideas from anywhere within the organization.

- Welcome ideas from outside of the organization and industry.

- Take concrete steps to begin establishing an organizational culture that actively supports innovation. This can begin with small steps, such as creating informal gathering areas, redecorating key areas to make them more conducive to creative thinking, holding open meetings to solicit input on the strategic direction of the organization, etc.

- Hold regular community building events during working hours. These might include lunchtime cookouts, mid-afternoon dessert breaks, disruptive moments, and light-hearted internal contests and competitions as well as celebrating company milestones resulting from innovation. Whenever possible, company leadership should be visibly involved in these events.

- Bring in outside high-content speakers who will challenge your employees to think in new ways.

- Allow your Giraffe innovators to set-aside a portion of their time to pursue innovation opportunities of their choice.

- Commit the needed resources to promising innovation initiatives.

- Establish the position of Chief Innovation Officer (CIO).

These are only a few suggestions of the kinds of changes which send a clear signal that the organization's leadership has made a real commitment to creating a culture where breakthrough innovation can become a driving force in the organization's future. This is the first step to re-engaging the Giraffes who remain on your *reserve*.

But what if there are no Giraffes left? Then, you must waste no time in searching for qualified individuals who can be persuaded to join your team. There are three strategies for finding Giraffes. First, the time-honored practice of rustling experienced Giraffes from other organizations. Touting an innovation friendly culture can be enticing bait for attracting Giraffes from wherever they may already be spinning straw into gold. Second, you can take your chances with bright, young people just entering the job market, or those who possess a few years of business experience, but have yet to function as Giraffes. This can be risky, but it is extremely rewarding to bring fledglings in on the ground floor and watch them move up through the organization learning its 'personality' as they go. A knowledge of 'how things really get done' can prove extremely useful down the road. Let's face it, in every organization there is the 'official' way and then, the 'black ops' way of making things happen. Both are important to know when moving innovation forward.

Lastly, cultivate your own from your existing senior leadership ranks. This is how I learned that I was a Giraffe. Early in my career, I worked for a company in the petroleum and petrochemical industry. I was responsible for all of the transportation and distribution functions nationally. I was also part of the seven member senior executive team. One day the company President, to whom I reported, met with me and announced that he and the chairman had made the decision that someone needed to be responsible for setting a strategic direction for the corporation's future. He proceeded to say that they had selected me for this position. This was long before anyone ever thought of using the word 'innovation' in a business context, much less a title such as Chief Innovation Officer.

I was shocked! What was I supposed to do? I was being asked to turn over all of my daily operational management responsibilities and retain only an advisory and trouble-shooting capacity over them. After transitioning, I decided that the first new market to target would be jet fuel for the airlines. This was a market I had been advocating for two years, but had met with opposition as the more seasoned company executives were convinced it was an impossible market to crack. I had also asked colleagues from other companies, both the major oil companies and the large independents, but they all echoed the same opinion.

For a new player to enter the business of selling Jet-A to major U.S. airlines, access was required not only to stable supplies of jet fuel and the petroleum pipelines serving the major airports, but as importantly to the fuel terminal facilities at those airports. At the time, this last component was viewed as an impossible task. The fuel supplies and pipeline capacity were not an issue. However, the terminal facilities were tightly controlled by a handful of major oil companies and airlines ever since the two earlier oil shocks of the 1970s, the airlines had been fiercely protective of their own fuel supplies and storage facilities.

When I informed the company president of my intent to find a way to enter the jet fuel business, he told me I would just be beating my head against a brick wall and advised me to instead choose something at which I could succeed as my first initiative. But after I persisted, he relented acknowledging that as the company strategist, I was free to try whatever I thought best, but (he added) when I failed, I needed to pick a better target market to grow the company. While he could not see the vision, he gave me a free reign to pursue the vision I had.

I singled out Chicago's O'Hare International airport, then the busiest U.S. airport, as an initial location to demonstrate the new airline marketing scenario I had been concocting. Approaching United Airlines (the dominant airline operating the most flights into and out of O'Hare), I proposed that United begin purchasing a small portion of their total Jet-A requirements from our company. As expected, United refused, querying how such a proposal could possibly benefit them.

I responded with an unprecedented offer — our company would supply fuel to United within an agreed upon monthly quantity range, at all times holding and making available a specified minimum quantity of fuel, partly in United's own O'Hare storage facility, with the balance in transit in the pipeline. In return, United would allow us to throughput agreed upon additional quantities of Jet-A through their storage at O'Hare and, in addition to the quantity of fuel we had committed to supply United for the month, we would guarantee a right of first refusal to United on each new pipeline tender (shipment). United Airlines wasted no time accepting the proposal.

Why did the airline undergo a sudden change of heart? Because at that time, United's primary concern was fuel security. After the two oil shocks of the 1970s, United's first priority was to ensure its supply of jet fuel, without which all of its airline operations could come to grinding halt — the worst possible scenario for any airline. United had come to equate fuel security with fuel ownership, but my innovative proposal changed that paradigm.

Through this agreement, United would not only maintain their current fuel security position, but improve it by gaining access to our company's fuel stocks in their terminal and the fuel transiting in the pipeline as well as that scheduled for shipment. In addition, United gained added throughput and inventory turns in its storage facility, thereby reducing its own throughput cost per gallon as well as its holding cost, since fuel purchased from our company was not invoiced until used.

We gained United Airlines as a new customer, while simultaneously obtaining access to Jet-A sales to all of the airlines at the nation's busiest airport which were previously totally inaccessible. I then proceeded to add Denver Airport, once again with United, as well as the three New York area airports (Kennedy, LaGuardia and Newark) partnering with TWA, each time relying upon the now proven technique of utilizing the airlines' storage facilities for a mutual strategic benefit.

When I brought in the initial contract with United Airlines, the company president just shook his head, asking what magic I had used to win them over. I replied, 'No magic, it was just a matter of understanding what their primary driver was in regard to fuel, in this case, 'security' and from there it was easy to construct a win-win scenario.'

So, yes, developing your own Giraffes can be very effective, if you choose them carefully and undergird them with the support they require. Whatever approach you decide to take, be sure to choose your Giraffes carefully. Thoroughly examine their track record. If it is someone within your company, are they already functioning as an out-of-the-box thinker, an innovator, in their current position? At the petroleum company, I had become known unofficially as the 'go-to-guy' for problem solving. In our executive team meetings, when discussion dragged on without a solution being reached, the president would invariably look over to me and say, 'John, I want you to solve this one.' On one occasion when we had deliberated an unusually long time over a particularly difficult problem he said to the executive team, 'We'll give it to John. He'll go away and when he comes back he'll have the answer we need.'

In one instance, after originating the concept, I had overseen the development of the first real time railcar tracking software in the nation. We were using it before the railroads. In order to achieve this, I had to fight our captive software programming company tooth and nail, as they could not understand the importance of real-time data versus periodic data updates. I won, and the results were hugely successful for the company.

In recruiting young people, college transcripts as well as resumes should be scrutinized and not by computerized screening programs. You may inadvertently screen out your future Giraffes. Look for academic achievements and awards. What did he or she excel in? The school that he or she attended need not have been Ivy League, but was the coursework rigorous? What else have they done? College internships? Have they served as community volunteers? What about interests, hobbies, and avocations? Have they traveled internationally? Are they readers? If so, what is their preferred reading material? What indicators of determination and character does the candidate evidence? Is he or she self-disciplined, mentally active and most of all, interesting?

At Zappos, all new hires are interviewed numerous times by groups of three or more people, sometimes off-site (over lunch) or after work (over a drink). This includes two distinct types of interviews. The first is for skills, whereas the second is purely cultural. Is the person a 'fit' for the Zappos culture? Prospective hires must pass both sets of interviews to be hired. The group interviews enable hiring teams to delve much deeper into what makes the applicant 'tick' as well as assessing interpersonal skills. The company hires only 1% of all applicants. Zappos also screens retroactively. Every new employee, even management and executive level hires, begins with a four-week training program that rotates them through the functions of the company. At the end of week one, new employees are offered a $2,000 buy-out if they want to quit — then and there. Zappos leadership understands that it is better to incentivize anyone who is not really a fit to leave on the front end, rather than having to deal with the consequences of an employee who does not match the overall company culture.

Once you know what you are looking for, there are many ways of seeking out Giraffes. Depending on the organizational level and function in question, these methods vary. At senior level management and executive positions, a recruiter is certainly the most typical, but not the only approach for filling positions. Another strategy is to become active in one of the many innovation forums found on the web. The ISPIM members group on LinkedIn is just one example of this. Periodicals such as *Innovation Magazine*, as well as other print and electronic media, innovation conferences and web blog sites are other resources for finding Giraffe innovators. There are over eleven thousand executives in the U.S. and Canada that have the word 'Innovation' in their title.

Understanding the essential characteristics to look for in a Giraffe places you well ahead of the curve in your search. In the interview process, openness and honesty are of critical importance. If your company is in transition, just now becoming aware of the difference Giraffes can make to your future, be candid about that fact. Candidates who do their research will likely ascertain this beforehand, but if they don't and discover the truth only after they come on board, the relationship between you may well be undermined from the outset. If you are working with a recruiter, be up front with them as well. It will make their search more efficient and likely result in better candidates being sent out.

Although they share certain common characteristics in regard to their ability to innovate, Giraffes, like any other employees, are still individuals. Some will be more experienced and competent to advise you in developing the organization's innovation efforts from scratch. These Giraffes welcome the challenge of starting from a clean slate, while others may be reticent, preferring, or even needing a more established support structure.

Carefully assess the internal opposition and resistance likely to arise; consider from what quarters it will originate. Choose Giraffes who have the confidence to 'stand the heat' and possess the requisite people skills to prevail without alienating their detractors, keeping in mind the objective of eventually winning them over since the results achieved will speak for themselves. If your innovation program is already well established, then select Giraffes better suited to taking the organization's existing strategy for innovation to the next level.

But don't limit your search for creatively talented individuals to the senior management and executive levels. Your organization will best benefit if Giraffes are present throughout all levels and functions. As I have noted, innovation is not the exclusive domain of R&D or engineering. Anything and everything that your organization either does now or seeks to do in the future should be scrutinized for the application of innovative thinking. Having Giraffes scattered throughout your organization will assure the steady flow of great ideas as the entire organization rises to the innovation imperative.

When seeking to add new personnel at any level, make certain that an attitude of openness to new ideas, creativity and change is a criterion interviewers are cognizant of and actively seeking. No organization needs or wants everyone to be a Giraffe, but having them well placed across the organization and immersed in a culture that is open to positive change will spur innovation and position your company on the starting grid, poised to run swiftly in the competitive race.

Giraffe Example:

Colonel John Boyd

If you define yourself as an expert, then you know everything and are unwilling to learn anything new. I will never take the mantle on as an expert because there is always something new to learn. Keep your mind open to new ideas. Harry Hillaker, who was a perfect example, embraced this concept and the F-16 and F-18 became a reality which at the time was unconceivable. Enough said!

John Boyd was a brilliant – though cantankerous, untidy, and foul-mouthed – cigar-smoking fighter pilot. While training new military pilots in the 1950s, he gained the moniker of '40-second Boyd' for offering $20 to any pilot who could evade him for more than 40 seconds in air-to-air combat maneuvers. No one ever succeeded. Later in his career, Boyd was instrumental in the conceptualization, design, and acceptance of the US Air Force's F-16 fighter aircraft. By the time of his death in 1997, he had also contributed invaluable safety expertise to the rule book on aerial combat tactics and overall warfare strategy.

While Air Force leadership was busy promoting the F-15 Eagle, their newest fighter, and the Navy was pushing the F-14 Tomcat, Boyd (also known as the 'Mad Major') and his colleagues (often referred to as the 'Fighter Mafia') conceived a smaller, lighter, and more agile fighter aircraft that could outperform both the F-15 and F-14. This aircraft also had a significantly lower life-cycle cost. Boyd proceeded to snatch a million dollars worth of Department of Defense computer time, giving his project various misleading titles and astutely slipping the developing concept past Air Force bureaucrats before they realized what they were authorizing. He stated, 'My goal was not personal. My work was for the best interest of the country. I tried to do it the Air Force Way and was refused at every turn. Then I did it my way.' Boyd's design resulted in the F-16, which has since become the most popular fighter aircraft in the world, currently in use in more than twenty nations.

According to biographer Robert Coram, Boyd's plot to develop the F-16, 'was one of the most audacious plots ever hatched against a military service and it was done under the noses of men who, if they had the slightest idea of what it was about, not only would have stopped it instantly, but would have cut orders reassigning Boyd to the other side of the globe.'

Jim Burton, a retired Air Force Colonel recalls how Boyd 'was the most intense man I've ever met or known.' He was so focused, Burton observes, that 'you could not communicate with him unless his mind was willing to allow that.' Likewise, Roger Franklin states that, Boyd 'demonstrates that radical change is possible, even in the world's most notoriously hidebound institution, the military, but suggests it must bubble up from deep within the ranks.' Former Defense Secretary Donald Rumsfeld called Boyd, 'The most influential military thinker since Sun Tzu wrote *The Art of War* 2400 years ago.' Boyd's indefatigable quest for excellence in aerial combat aircraft should be regarded as a touchstone for practical innovation in any setting.

Chapter 9 — Thought Questions

1. Do you now know what to look for in your search for Giraffes?

2. Do you think our organization has any Giraffes that have been in hiding? If so, do you have a plan to bring them in out of the cold?

3. If our organization has been hostile or simply indifferent to Giraffe innovators, what concrete action steps can be taken to send a 'believable' message to our Giraffe(s) that the climate has permanently changed in their favor?

4. How will our organization communicate that it is acceptable to take reasonable risks when innovating and that we understand that not all innovations efforts will succeed?

5. How will 'No Blame' after action reviews identify and positively communicate the lessons learned from failed innovation efforts to others involved in leading innovation, so that the organization can learn from and not repeat the same mistakes?

6. Which methods are best for our organization at this time, for recruiting, identifying and/or developing the needed Giraffe innovators?

7. What aspects of our organization's hiring practices need to change in order to ensure that new hires at all levels and positions will be people who are flexible and willing to embrace change and innovation?

8. Does our organization have any people in key positions who will hinder the transformation into a culture of innovation? How will the senior leadership deal with this opposition?

9. Was Col. John Boyd right in disguising his project to design the F-16 fighter aircraft and literally 'stealing' a million dollars of Department of Defense computer time to accomplish his goal?

10. What can we learn from Boyd's determination and unconventional methods of ramrodding the innovations that have forever changed aerial warfare and undoubtedly saved the lives of countless U.S. and allied combat pilots?

11. Roger Franklin states that, Boyd 'demonstrates that radical change is possible...but suggests it must bubble up from deep within the ranks'. How important is it in any organization that innovation 'bubble up from deep within?'

Breakthrough innovation opens our minds to a world of possibilities.

Chapter Ten: The Giraffe Advantage

Giraffa camelopardalis is a Latin derivation of the Greek name for this animal species. While it has been abbreviated to *giraffe*, the original Greek word lives on in the constellation 'Camelopardalis' named by Dutch astronomer and theologian, Petrus Plancius. Visible in the northern hemisphere, this giraffe-shaped constellation boasts several remarkable double star systems, but its brightest star is Beta Cam.

Convinced that you need the magic touch of one or more Giraffes? Breakthrough innovation opens our minds to a world of possibilities. Think like a Giraffe and discover the dynamic that will forever change the future of your organization.

But Giraffes are not the 'whole package.' Excellent, leadership is paramount to the success of innovation. Nevertheless, Giraffes possess the unique blend of vision, creativity and critical thinking skills essential for creating the innovative initiatives that will ensure sustainability. Giraffes create the kick-off with insights and daring ideas so that people with more functionally-oriented skill sets are able to 'pick up the ball and run,' implementing and expediting those innovations. It may take only one individual to conceive and define a blockbuster innovation, but it takes a team to bring it to reality – a team determined to battle time and tide in developing new products destined, according to Steve Jobs, 'to change history.'

The brainchild of two Giraffes, Apple was to revolutionize the (1) personal computing, (2) graphic arts, (3) movie animation, (4) music, (5) cell phone,

(6) digital publishing and (7)tablet computing industries. Steve Jobs, the big picture visionary whose concepts resulted in market-shattering ideas and Steve Wozniak, the technical genius who transformed those ideas into something others could actualize, had founded the company. While worlds apart in mindsets, skill sets and personalities, both were brilliant innovators. But even that was not enough. For sustainable success, they recognized the need to create an exciting culture of innovation where teams of very bright, highly motivated people would propel raw ideas into spectacular innovations.

What is the strategic vision for your organization? Will you reach for *change that creates new dimensions of performance?* Can you picture development teams of gifted and motivated individuals free to function synergistically within your organization?

Begin by creating an environment which inspires and challenges teams to attempt what appears impossible. Breakthrough innovation flourishes when Giraffe driven projects – aided by cohesive development teams with common goals, passionate commitment and complementary strengths – develop a synergistic capacity for innovation. Defying the status quo, they collaborate relentlessly until optimal solutions are found. Organizations that have established this dynamic realize the exponential rewards of the 'Giraffe Advantage': on-going strategic innovation.

Why not reach for the stars? Good intentions won't reposition you in the marketplace, but decisive action will. Perhaps, you are old enough to remember the classic space adventure series, Star Trek? Each episode began with a narrative defining the mission of the Starship Enterprise: '... to explore strange, new worlds, to seek out new life and new civilizations, to boldly go where no one has gone before.' Innovation either *is* or *is not* the 'prime directive' of your organization. You cannot 'make it so' (as Star Trek: The Next Generation Starfleet Captain Jean Luc Picard, was known to say) by merely giving the command. Breakthrough innovation requires top-down commitment and concerted effort.

The original Star Trek series may have lasted only three years (1966-69), but it left an indelible mark on America's youth. Teeming with wildly creative concepts, it inspired the imagination of an entire generation to explore 'new worlds' in science and technology. The results can be seen today: the Star Trek communicator was realized in the iPhone and the Padd became our iPad. Today, Vocera produces a communicator badge and the Stand Off Triage Tool (TriCorder) used by Dr. McCoy to check vital signs is currently being developed by the U.S. military.

Take the leap. Commit to changing the culture of your organization into one that embraces creativity and fosters an environment where not only Giraffes, but everyone will thrive. Overcome fear. While it cannot be denied that risk is a factor in all innovation, the truth is: 'no pain, no gain.' Consider the alternative: the failure to innovate will ultimately result in your organization's decline and eventual demise. Essential changes must precede the achievement of desired results. Depending on how open or closed your organization is today, it may take time to win people over, build bridges, and regain the trust that has been lost.

Virtually everyone wants to be part of something larger than themselves, something of intrinsic value that will make the world a better place. Innovate to become a marketplace leader. Foster a culture of innovation and guard it fiercely.

If space is the 'Final Frontier,' then innovation is the 'Final Strategy.' It is your passport to the future. Now is the time to innovate. Whole new worlds await you! Begin by...

Minding the Giraffes!

Giraffe Example:

Thomas Fogarty, MD

Identifying needs is the first impetus...Current (medical device) technology is rarely developed by one person. It's developed by a team.

Dr. Thomas Fogarty has acted as a driving force in medical device innovation for nearly 40 years. He founded or co-founded more than 33 medical device companies and is named on more than 150 patents for medical devices, among them the Fogarty balloon embolectomy catheter, which revolutionized vascular surgery.

Fogarty is a cardiovascular surgeon, inventor, and 2012 MDEA Lifetime Achievement Award Winner. The Medical Device Excellence Awards event, the industry's premier awards ceremony for medical device design and innovation, honored Dr. Fogarty with this prestigious award for his outstanding accomplishments in the medical device industry. At the awards ceremony, Dean Kamen, himself a recipient of the Lifetime Achievement Award, recalled the following: 'In my early days, Dr. Fogarty was kind of the poster child for an innovator in technology and now that I have gotten to know him over the years, he deserves that reputation.' Humbly accepting the award, Dr. Fogarty made a point of thanking his patients. Standing before a capacity audience of medical device professionals, he said, 'Probably the real heroes of innovation of the medical device industry and drug industry are our patients. Those are the ones willing to take a risk and allow us to evaluate new technology and new drugs in themselves.'

While still a teenager, Fogarty re-invented a centrifugal clutch. Then, while working as a scrub technician at a Cincinnati hospital during medical school, Fogarty used a surgical glove, in conjunction with tying techniques that he had learned from fly-fishing, to design what became the embolectomy balloon catheter, the first minimally invasive surgical device. The catheter remains in common use today. Prior to its invention, up to 50% of patients either died or lost limbs during surgeries to remove blood clots.

Fogarty was on the surgical team that performed the first heart transplant surgery in the United States. With over 100 surgical patents, Dr. Fogarty is one of the most prolific medical device inventors of all time. In 2000, he was awarded the Lemelson-MIT Prize for Invention and Innovation. And in 2001, he was the recipient of the Jacobson Innovation Award of the American College of Surgeons, and he was inducted into the National Inventors' Hall of Fame that same year. He also founded the Thomas Fogarty Institute for Innovation in 2007.

Fogarty credits his success to persistence and an ardent refusal to give up. He always asks himself: 'How can I make this better? How can I reduce pain? How can I get the patient out of the hospital more quickly?' His 'patient first' priority is evident in statements such as, 'You'd have a hard time finding anyone saying that I was more interested in money than in the patient.' A Giraffe with a mission, Thomas Fogarty's medical innovations have saved the lives of millions of people worldwide.

Chapter 10 — Thought Questions

1. Does our organization have the crucial combination of Giraffes and strong, committed, supportive leadership in place to create the essential culture of innovation?

2. Apple's two founders provided the complementary skill sets of the big picture marketplace strategy and hands-on make-it-happen innovation. Does our organization possess both aspects of innovation through one or more Giraffes?

3. Is our organization's culture one which supports and fosters synergistic collaboration across organizational lines or do individual fiefdoms block cooperation?

4. Is 'impossible' a word that stops us dead in our tracks and causes us to back track and change direction or does it challenge us to create *what can be?*

5. Are 'status quo' and 'safe' words that aptly describe our organization's approach to doing business?

6. Do we agree that, *Essential changes must precede the achievement of desired results?*

7. Does our organization regularly offer our people the opportunity to be, *Part of something larger than themselves, something of intrinsic value that will make the world a better place?*

8. Do we agree with the statement that: *Innovation is the final strategy?* Why or why not?

9. What does Dr. Thomas Fogarty's use of fly fishing knots in creating the embolectomy balloon catheter demonstrate about successful innovation?

10. Dr. Fogarty credits his success to persistence and an ardent refusal to give up. He always asks himself: *How can I make this better?* Is this a driving motivation demonstrated by our senior leadership team and reflected throughout our organization? Does our organization view the *hot pursuit* of innovation as the way to make things better?

It is vital to the innovation effort that everyone be onboard, playing one game, on one team, with one purpose and shared goal.

An Innovation Triumph

Successful innovation always begins with a good idea and a commitment to accomplish something of tangible value. This is the story of a think outside-the-box solution which rescued a great product from certain death, thus demonstrating the value of simple, well-executed and courageous innovation.

Imagine for a moment a company, a once dominant leader in its market category with a huge following and very catchy jingle, the kind of tune that you find yourself singing or whistling unconsciously. But over the course of many years, its marketing is neglected and its product line allowed to age, languish and very nearly disappear.

What can be done when it's already too late? The normal strategy would be to kill the brand and introduce a new one to take its place — actually 'safer' and probably more cost effective over the long run than trying to revive an almost dead brand.

Fortunately, that's not what happened. The brand? None other than that venerable ladies' cologne, 'Old Spice.' Yes, that's what I said – *ladies'* brand. Old Spice began life in 1937 as a ladies' cologne under the label, 'Early American Old Spice.' Then, in a strategic reversal, Old Spice was reintroduced as a scent for men in 1938. Through the 1950s and into the 1960s, it was a staple of most American men's shaving kits. Growing up, I can remember the distinctive cream-colored glass bottle on the bathroom shelf, frequently used by my father and older brother.

By the 1970s, times were changing and a bevy of trendy new colognes appeared on the scene: Brut, British Sterling, Jade East and English Leather, to name but a few. The hold of Old Spice was finally broken and the brand spiraled into a long period of decline. By 2010, what little customer base remained consisted of men in mid-life and older.

In 1990, the brand was sold to Procter and Gamble (P&G). Then, in 2006, P&G commissioned an advertising agency, Wieden + Kennedy, to recast the Old Spice image so that it would appeal to a younger clientele, particularly the Gen Y target market. In the brilliant stroke of a single Super Bowl advertisement in 2010, the handsome and irresistibly charming former pro football player, Isaiah Mustafa, became an overnight sensation as the 'Old Spice Man.'

This was followed by a television advertising campaign targeting programs young couples were likely to watch together. In the first quarter of 2010, Old Spice captured 75% of all conversations in the market category, with over half of the buzz generated by women. TV programs such as Oprah also spotlighted the phenomenon.

Crowning this marketing triumph, the following message was posted on Twitter five months later: 'Today could be just like the other 364 days you log into Twitter, or maybe the Old Spice Man shows up @OldSpice.' Thus began 'The Response Campaign' for Old Spice men's body wash. As people began posting questions, the 'Old Spice Man' responded with real time answers in a massive social media blitz which included 186 YouTube videos with Mustafa starring in every one of them, sometimes wearing a bath towel, as, 'The Man Your Man Could Smell Like.' In just two and a half days of filming, Mustafa responded to questions posted by both fans and celebrities on Twitter, Facebook and other social media platforms. The campaign was facilitated by a talented team of social media experts who, in real time, analyzed individual questions and quickly scripted clever responses for the 'Old Spice Man' to deliver. The more videos they posted, the more questions rained in.

Old Spice Man's foxy comebacks, posted on YouTube, sparked the fastest growing and most popular interactive social media campaign in history. On the first day, it generated 5.9 million views. On the second day, Old Spice had eight of the top eleven most popular videos on the web. By the third day, the campaign had generated more than 20 million views. By the end of the first week, there had been over 40 million views of these videos, an astounding success in social media advertising. As remarkable as this is, it was no flash in the pan; in the first six months after the videos appeared, over 1.4 billion impressions were generated!

Most importantly, the Old Spice demographic dramatically shifted with the product becoming not only accepted, but sought after by Gen Y men and women, as women are the primary purchasers of these products for the men in their lives. In that same six-month period, sales of Old Spice Body Wash increased 27% over the previous year, up 55% in the second three-month period and 107% in the last month, making Old Spice the number one brand of men's body wash.

P&G has continued building upon this marketing success by creating videos aimed at young men as well as the women who strongly influence men's decisions in this product category. The video campaign has continued to escalate with the addition of more 'Old Spice Men' in varying themes.

Nor has P&G ignored product packaging opportunities that promote an aura of masculinity. For example, while keeping the original design of the cologne bottle (in plastic now, rather than glass), the box is now inscribed with these words: **'IF YOUR GRANDFATHER HADN'T WORN IT, YOU WOULDN'T EXIST. Cool, crisp and clean. The unmistakably masculine scent of Old Spice.'**

Drop the fatigued, aging brand and start all over? Why, when a simple dose of well-orchestrated innovation is all that was necessary? It is interesting to note P&G's initial use of a single Super Bowl ad as the launch medium for initiating a much broader advertising campaign. Others have done the same with great success, breaking the longstanding advertising rule of not placing single run ads. In 1984, Apple announced the first Macintosh computer using a single, literally smashing (i.e., female jogger flinging a sledge hammer) ad at the Super Bowl and, in 1999, Victoria's Secret followed suit, to announce its first web-streamed fashion show.

Rules must sometimes be shattered to outwit the competition and produce leap-ahead market breakthroughs. Remember, there is no limit to what the imagination can devise. For Giraffes, anything is possible. The quest of a true Giraffe is to realize *what can be!*

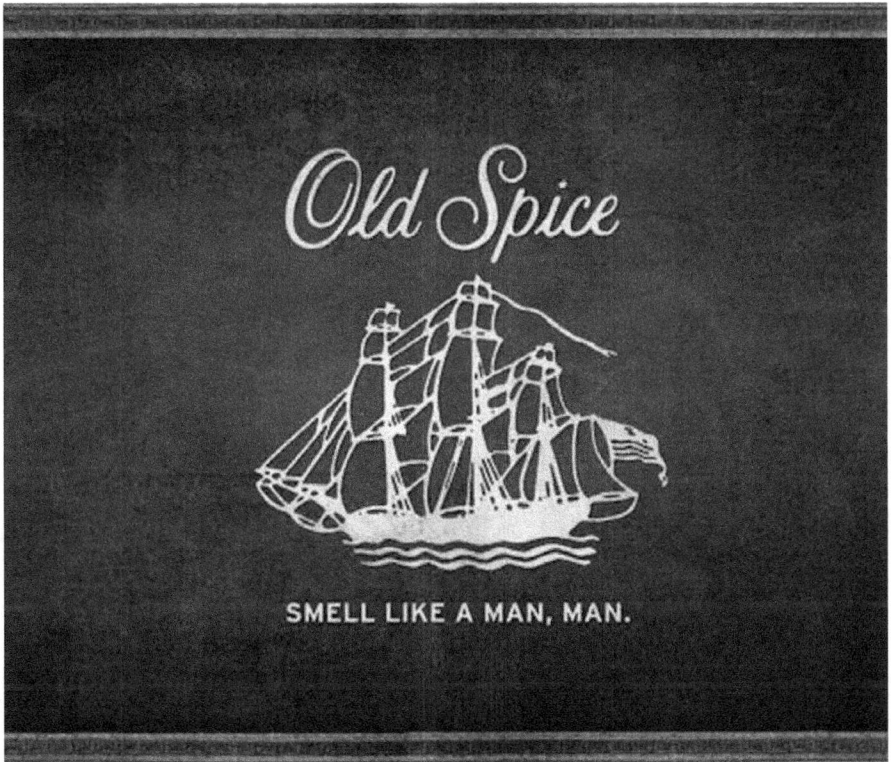

SMELL LIKE A MAN, MAN.

Old Spice and the Old Spice Logo are registered Trademarks of Procter & Gamble

Innovation is the act of creating something with purpose.... bringing new value to the organization.

The World's Best Loved Giraffe

Sophie is indisputably the world's best loved giraffe. In fact, she is a worldwide celebrity. Sophie also happens to be made of rubber. If you have small children, are a grandparent, or happen to know people with babies, then you may have already been introduced to Sophie.

Recognized internationally, Sophie is an adorable, 7" high, additive-free, natural rubber Giraffe that was first created in 1961 as a toddler's teething toy. She has hand-painted brown spots, rosy pink cheeks, and black eyes. Sophie squeaks softly when squeezed by little hands.

Sophie is a native of France, produced exclusively in a small batch process by an Alpine factory. She has become a full-scale international tradition. While other teethers are typically priced around $5 retail, Sophie commands the surprising price of $25 in the U.S., selling in high-end stores worldwide. Interestingly, in France, Sophie is priced at the equivalent of about $12 and merchandised in retail blister pack, point-of-purchase displays in grocery stores nationwide. Price notwithstanding, Sophie is clearly the teether of choice.

In a world where branded children's products abound, this uniquely simple rubber teether has risen to celebrity status with surprising alacrity. Vulli S.A.S., the originator and manufacturer of Sophie, has annual sales of €22 million (nearly $30 million USD). Although export sales did not begin in earnest until 2007, the company expects to sell more product outside of France than domestically in 2012. Building on the mystique and perceived upscale image of French products, Vulli has benefited by selling Sophie internationally in attractive bio-degradable boxes that feature an image of the Eiffel Tower.

Although this represents an astonishing number of unit sales for a very high priced teether, the true scope of Sophie's success can be better gauged by the 2010 domestic sales in France, where Sophie reached 816,000 units sold in a country where only 828,000 babies were born!

Why is this toy giraffe so popular? To begin with, Sophie connects with all five of a child's senses: sight (appealing colors), hearing (the muted squeak), taste (she is easily gnawed, soothing babies with sore gums), touch (pliable and easy to hold shape), and smell (there is something reassuring about the aroma of natural rubber).

At a time when scores of children's products, many of which are manufactured in China for major western companies, have been recalled for contamination from lead and other heavy metals or similarly dangerous compounds, Vulli has maintained strict control over manufacturing by keeping their product line internal. Even the manufacturing process is innovative, employing natural materials, with casting molds made of plaster. The promise of a safe, natural (non-plastic), high quality and environmentally-friendly toy creates a widespread consumer readiness to pay premium prices.

Building on their remarkable international success, Vulli is expanding the Sophie product line with new additions, including the So'Pure line of organic blankets, teethers and rattles. Vulli's choice of natural rubber as their raw material helps to insulate Sophie from the competition, as it requires manual, high-skill, small batch production methods versus the mass production techniques used with plastics. Vulli CEO Serge Jacquemier says that he isn't open to new ways to make Sophie. Sophie products 'must be irreproachable.'

As stated earlier, the speed of the leader determines the rate of the pack! People will not outstrip the performance of their leadership. Vulli's CEO has led his organization to astounding success through an unswerving commitment to maintaining the highest standards in the production of this innovative toy. He had a vision and held to it. Sustainable profitability is the natural outcome.

Sophie

Sophie the giraffe is a product of Vulli S.A.S

You have to be run by ideas, not hierarchy. The best ideas have to win.

- *Steve Jobs*

He [Steve Jobs] would think out new ways of doing things and do it in a totally different way that the world would swing toward.

- *Steve Wozniak*

For his achievements, Steve Wozniak was awarded the National Medal of Technology by then President Ronald Reagan in 1985. This is the highest honor bestowed on an American innovator. In 2000, he was inducted into the Inventors Hall of Fame and awarded the prestigious Heinz Award for Technology, the Economy and Employment.

We can't solve problems by using the same kind of thinking we used when we created them.

– Albert Einstein

Parting Thought Question

What *tangible actions* will you and your organization take as a result of reading *Minding the Giraffes: The People Side of Innovation?*

For More Information

To learn more about John's innovation consulting and keynote speaking programs, visit the following websites:

MindingTheGiraffes.com

RedDoorInnovation.com

DiFrances.com

Or contact John at: Contact@DiFrances.com

www.ingramcontent.com/pod-product-compliance
Lightning Source LLC
Chambersburg PA
CBHW072222270326
41930CB00010B/1957